KARATE
KINEMATICS
AND
DYNAMICS

UNIQUE
PUBLICATIONS

7011 SUNSET BLVD., HOLLYWOOD, CALIF. 90028

PREFACE

Many of the concepts in Part I of this book have already appeared in my previous book, *The Karate Instructor's Handbook,* published in 1976 by the Institute for the Study of Attention, a subsidiary of Physical Studies Institute. I had hoped that this book would motivate others to contribute similar technical books and papers to the body of karate knowledge, but I have been disappointed. There is no rigorous collection of writings comparable to most other physical disciplines.

Instructors learn from their mistakes and successes, and I too have learned much since writing that book. So, when Daniel Furuya of Unique Publications contacted me, and asked if I would be interested in writing another karate book, I jumped at the opportunity. He shares my vision that true disciplines require bona fide, creative and thorough research, and that more martial arts books are necessary to translate these ideas into practical teaching methodologies. He has also shared much of the work necessary to create this book.

I thank all my students, past and present, for sharing the experiences necessary for me to create the teaching methodology expounded in this book. Dennis Dean, a 2nd Dan Black Belt, and Steve Ramsdell, an eleven year old 1st Dan Jr. Black Belt appear with me in some of the photographs. I also thank Cindy Ramage and Stuart Smith for helping me type some of the the manuscript into a word processor, and Margaret Kahn, Linda Montano and Louis Seitchik for helping with the final editing. I was then able to straightforwardly do the typesetting at Physical Studies Institute.

With regards to my primary emphases on physics and attention, none of my previous teachers or training comrades from 1958 and previous to 1970, when I started my own school, gave any appreciable contribution to the formulation or application of the ideas expressed in this book. I respect them for the integrity they may demonstrate in their own art, but I trust they are not disappointed with the absence of any further acknowledgements. It would also be inappropriate for me to use their specific names and positions merely to promote my work. I expect that mutual benefits already derived from our previous interactions are sufficient rewards. Of course, I savor the additional satisfaction and responsibility of "doing it my way." I hope other instructors will view this book as a challenge to commit their own ideas to writing, for others to try and test.

Lester Ingber
Physical Studies Institute
Drawer W
Solana Beach, CA 92075
July, 1981

CONTENTS

PART II. TRAINING DYNAMICS

PART III. LIVING DYNAMICS

INTRODUCTION

A. General Philosophy

Karate and other martial arts appeal to men and women of all ages, whose interests range among: self-defense, competition, form (kata), discipline, and physical exercise. Many people sense that these body disciplines permit an efficient access to enhanced body awareness and an appreciation of quite generally pervasive meditative aspects of interacting with one's internal and external environments. Many of these aspects are quite common to other physical and cognitive disciplines, including fine arts and academics.

To accomplish any of the above general aspects offered by karate training, it is necessary to develop a specific language and set of tools for study. There is no substitute for correct, rigorous and disciplined training over a period of many years to achieve the dynamic power, flexibility, endurance, and skilled technique and awareness necessary for peak performance in karate -- identical to requirements in any bona fide discipline!

A course of study that is organized to clearly present and rigorously teach the essential body kinematics and dynamics of natural movement using sound principles of physics -- production of forces, momentum and energy -- will increase the efficiency of learning karate and general body awareness. This is simply because these principles have been developed to be the most concise and accurate description of kinematics and dynamics of physical movement. Of course, to be useful these concepts must be naturally integrated with the context of the specific discipline as part of the regular training. Similarly, a course of study that practically and rigorously promotes attentional skills -- rhythms, awareness of spaces between techniques, strategic possibilities -- by giving attentional feedback as an intimate, explicit component of regular training will also increase the efficiency of developing awareness of one's environment. At the same time, it will promote learning the skills necessary to appropriately interact with optimum strategy, rhythm and timing.

Since 1958, when I first started my own karate training, I have continually attempted to formulate and refine a course of instruction to accomplish the above tasks. I have noted that in body disciplines, as in academics, there are relatively few truly gifted people. Fewer of these "geniuses" are aware of the source of their talents, and even fewer are interested and aware of how to teach others to acquire their skills. Indeed, too often, leaders and teachers in our educational institutions, although usually directly or indirectly paid by the general public, believe it is not possible to teach an "average person" their skills. Whether this takes the form of an arrogant or a patronizing attitude, this is still clearly nonsense. The task of a good teacher is to set a path on which the average student, obviously most students, may become creative, limited only by his or her will and perseverance to succeed.

Interestingly, when precise specific physical and attentional skills clearly form the basis and goals of karate study, the regular practice assumes a creative and constructive context, rather than a paranoid and destructive context that is often promoted by goals specifically oriented to self-defense, although the same skills are required for either set of goals. No extraneous cultural or formally religious setting is necessary. Sexism, racism, nationalism are irrelevant at best and destructive at worst to the serious pursuit of excellence. The implicit optimism I have is that if people are encouraged to rigorously and creatively develop their own physical and attentional capabilities, desirable attitudes defined by common reason will also develop, but within each one's own chosen cultural and religious setting. Often one's emotions, fixations and attitudes form obstacles to be overcome, as they are exposed in the constantly demanding and stressful class environment. These must be worked through before the student is fit to further develop by sparring, which requires using another person's body and mind to learn. Eventually, strong, fast and precise sparring becomes an ultimate tool to investigate, test and improve body and attentional skills. This is the worthy purpose to pursue training, and the purpose for society to foster such training in its individuals.

You will learn most deeply and efficiently if you give full commitment to all your techniques, and give similar respect to all your class opponents. You can learn something from everyone, and strategies and techniques must be tested to be workable with all opponents. Treat each mistake, they will be countless, as a death. Take each opportunity to live to try again, not to rehash an old error, but to attempt a new correct interaction. In this light, true competition is your best teacher, as long as it does not become perverted by undesirable emotions and attitudes. You test each interpersonal interaction, and quickly pounce on mistakes. The goal is to interact; the means is trying to win. If you are honest with yourself, you may often be winning, but still falling short of worthier goals, and thus, truly losing. This is a harder, but truer and more educational way to practice. Having only the goal being to win, and the means being beating on your classmate like some screaming psychopath out of a comic strip becomes a fruitless and frustrating pursuit in the final analysis.

As you appreciate more and more the concept, that the activity of karate necessitates continual interaction, your attitude towards techniques will completely change. For example, at first, at any given time, you are necessarily preoccupied with just doing a single body technique correctly. You are also trying to learn many body techniques. But body techniques can too easily become the focus of your study. STOP! This internal focus is as counterproductive as exclusively focusing on your opponent. Eventually, it will be a severe shock to face an opponent, as you try to throw up a disjointed vocabulary of blocks, punches, kicks, and strikes.

No doubt, you must do powerful techniques. At a beginner level most of your time is spent practicing techniques, at a more advanced level most of your real time is spent in motion, between consummating techniques, either in the process of leading to a technique, or in the process of controlling power from a previous technique. You must start as early as possible thinking in terms of fluid motion, of dynamic change from technique to technique, instead of statically locking your mind into thinking of making "magic" jumps from technique to technique. This attitude is possible to achieve even at the beginner level by truly appreciating the kinematics of individual techniques. By understanding the optimum beginning, middle and end of a given technique, you can also understand the best way to enter or leave that technique, and thereby to connect it to other techniques. Loss of these vital connections is truly synonymous with death. You must learn to sustain life in your karate activity from the very beginning, and to be dissatisfied with unwarranted breaks in this interaction.

At first, you will only realize these continually changing dynamic connections by making large overt body movements. Undoubtedly, you will at first be awkward and clumsy. But in this way you will see your mistakes and learn. If you stand still you will not learn. Eventually, after only a few years of practice, roughly the same span of time spent in any kind of school, you will be able to feel these dynamic fluxes, even when your opponent sometimes perceives you as motionless! At this stage of your training, for some fleeting instants, you will be able to control the flow of tensions in your body, being ready for motion, covertly capturing the sensation of motion itself. Further, at this level of perfected technique, you will sometimes be able to effectively "feint," to broadcast a full upcoming technique to your opponent, causing him or her to react, without actually fully committing yourself to that technique, but rather pursuing a better strategy. At this stage you are becoming fluent in the language of karate.

B. Organization of Book

A "technique" is defined in this book as a specific skill, like a punch, which has been researched and practiced for many years by many independent people, to the point where it is reasonable to require its study in a course of instruction. The course offered in this book includes a minimum division of three levels of practice. A beginner's class has a four-week cycle, an intermediate class has a thirteen-week cycle, and an advanced class offers ongoing sparring and kata practice. Students are expected to practice at least two to three one-hour class sessions per week. Eligibility for the advanced class typically requires at least one year's practice. After three to five years, the average persevering student is usually ready for strong fast and precise sparring. Before then, all exercise and sparring is centrally supervised in a disciplined, but progressive class environment. The general method of learning is to exercise large, overt body and attentional movements, enhancing immediate feedback and learning from one's incorrect as well as correct techniques. The particular Shotokan style of body techniques used in this book readily permits this methodology. However, it should become clear that the body and attentional principles described here are applicable to all karate styles, and to other body disciplines as well.

Part I of this book gives essential preliminaries and skills. These are used in Part II in specific training schedules that will take you through the above cycles of practice. Part III discusses a larger context of the purpose of training.

Chapter IA describes the kinematics of body movement. Kinematics is defined here to mean the study of how power is produced in individual body techniques, quite independent of one's personal state of size, weight, attention, or attitude. This is somewhat different from the physics and dictionary definitions, in that some dynamics of power production during techniques are also included. However, the definition used here is quite precise and useful for the purposes of this book, which is to also clarify the physical and mental dynamics responsible for connecting strings of techniques. Therefore, roughly speaking, kinematics will here deal with body techniques, and dynamics will here deal with connections between techniques.

Mastery of these concepts is essential. For karate students there are potentially tens of thousands of clearly defined techniques. By better understanding how all these techniques use only a few common physical principles, the student can more easily learn to make creative and spontaneous associations among techniques. Sparring is much like a dialogue between people. Creative, spontaneous associations are necessary in any language for effective communication and interaction. For people interested in other martial arts or physical disciplines, this chapter will detail similarities in movement. Aikido, ballet, judo, karate, and t'ai chi all use similar physical principles to varying degrees. By better understanding these similarities, with the use of a common language of physics designed for such description, you can also better appreciate their differences and strengths. For example, John Bryant, Kurt Rosi, Louis Seitchik, all karate black belts and tennis players, and myself, have written a book on the kinematics and dynamics of tennis, using the same methodology presented in this book: *Tennis Dynamics*, by Physical Studies Institute, is published by Unique Publications. We are also preparing *Ballet — The Art Defined*, by Louise Frazer.

With confidence and assurance, I can state that this learning methodology is not beyond anyone's grasp. It is not necessary to fully understand all the concepts in this chapter to learn the relatively few body feelings discussed. For example, besides regularly teaching an adult class, I have an ongoing children's class, ages 5 to 11 years old. They also study the course outlined in Part II, and readily grasp this methodology.

Chapter IB presents the basic body kinematics specific to karate techniques: stance, punching, blocking, striking, and kicking.

Chapter IC discusses attention dynamics. As this study must also take into account your opponent, these dynamics are more properly understood as interactions between people. This chapter gives explicit karate exercises to practice, to demonstrate the nature of the attentional states you are required to master to become proficient in karate, or in just about any discipline.

Part II presents courses of study that have been tested for many years. These courses include the above concepts as an intimate part of regular practice, going beyond giving lip service to lofty abstractions.

Chapter IIA, Beginner Dynamics, outlines a four-week beginner's course of study. There is also one Introductory class to acquaint the novice with some of the physical and attentional principles involved. This class also sets up a personal interaction with the advanced student giving this tutorial. Most people take this four-week cycle two to four times before being able to enter the next intermediate level. Many intermediate and advanced students often take this class as a continual refresher for basic techniques.

Chapter IIB, Intermediate Dynamics, outlines an intermediate course of study. After successfully completing the beginner's course, the student may enter during the first, fifth, or ninth week of the intermediate course. This course stresses body and attentional dynamics as defined above.

The thirteenth week of the quarter is exam week. Examples of written and physical exams. Many times students want to train this week as well, and many instructors may wish to complement this course with other special training, such as t'ai chi, weapons, etc. As a couple of examples, I have included self-defense and "stick-sparring" for this last week of the quarter. This is also a good time to have a more rigorous special seminar for a week or weekend.

Chapter IIC, Advanced Dynamics, outlines an advanced course of study. Typically, all colored belts (after about one year's practice) can take this class immediately after warming up in the intermediate class. After doing special control and timing exercises, the class can break into two parts, for fast and slow free-sparring. Instructors should use their common sense, not a specific belt color, to determine whether a student should do fast or slow free-sparring. Only at or above 2nd Dan black belt can one assume that a student should always do the fast free-sparring.

Part III is a personal perspective on how karate training fits into a larger context of individual and societal consciousness. This subject is of interest to many students, but it is also important to those people who feel it is unwarranted to attempt to generally extend a specialized activity into other activities. I agree that it is unwarranted to extend the "structure" of karate to other activities, for example pretending that all of life is one big Samurai game. However, I do not believe it is unwarranted to extend the "process" of learning and practicing karate to other activities. This process is essentially composed of the skills described here as attention dynamics, discussed in Chapter IC and explicitly applied throughout this book.

At first, you may only train in class several hours a week. If you learn to appreciate that the body and attentional dynamics practiced in class are also present outside of class, you immediately have the opportunity of practicing karate all day and all night! Perseverance and practice determine the ultimate level you will attain, and the more you can practice, the more certain you can be of attaining excellence, no matter your starting level. Similarly, you can learn to appreciate your karate training as a regularly scheduled, intensified experience to study these processes, so that you can better function in other aspects of your life. This was, and still is, my original motivation for studying karate. I hope it becomes yours.

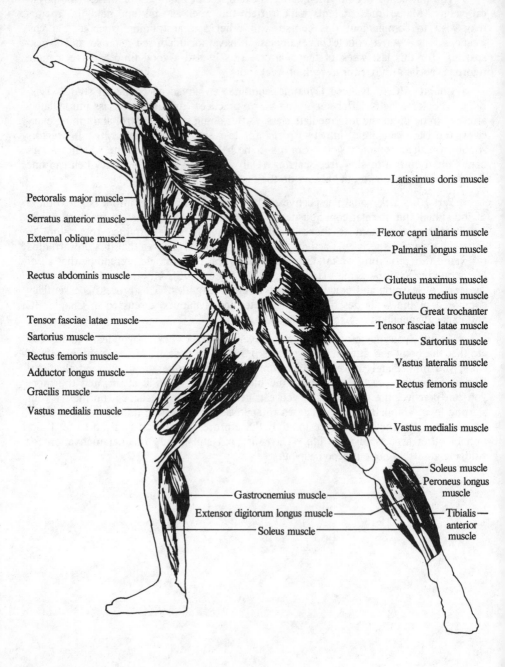

Latissimus doris muscle

Pectoralis major muscle

Serratus anterior muscle

External oblique muscle

Flexor capri ulnaris muscle

Palmaris longus muscle

Rectus abdominis muscle

Gluteus maximus muscle

Gluteus medius muscle

Great trochanter

Tensor fasciae latae muscle

Tensor fasciae latae muscle

Sartorius muscle

Sartorius muscle

Rectus femoris muscle

Vastus lateralis muscle

Adductor longus muscle

Rectus femoris muscle

Gracilis muscle

Vastus medialis muscle

Vastus medialis muscle

Soleus muscle

Peroneus longus muscle

Gastrocnemius muscle

Extensor digitorum longus muscle

Tibialis anterior muscle

Soleus muscle

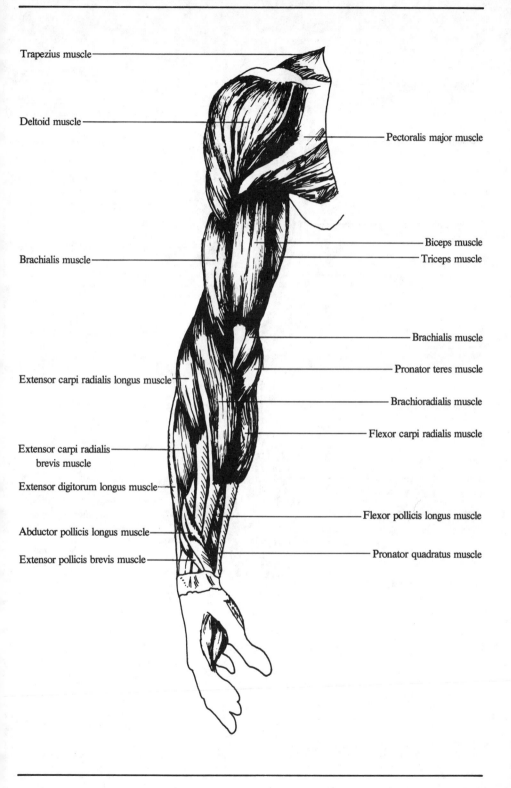

Trapezius muscle

Deltoid muscle

Pectoralis major muscle

Biceps muscle

Triceps muscle

Brachialis muscle

Brachialis muscle

Pronator teres muscle

Extensor carpi radialis longus muscle

Brachioradialis muscle

Flexor carpi radialis muscle

Extensor carpi radialis
brevis muscle

Extensor digitorum longus muscle

Flexor pollicis longus muscle

Abductor pollicis longus muscle

Pronator quadratus muscle

Extensor pollicis brevis muscle

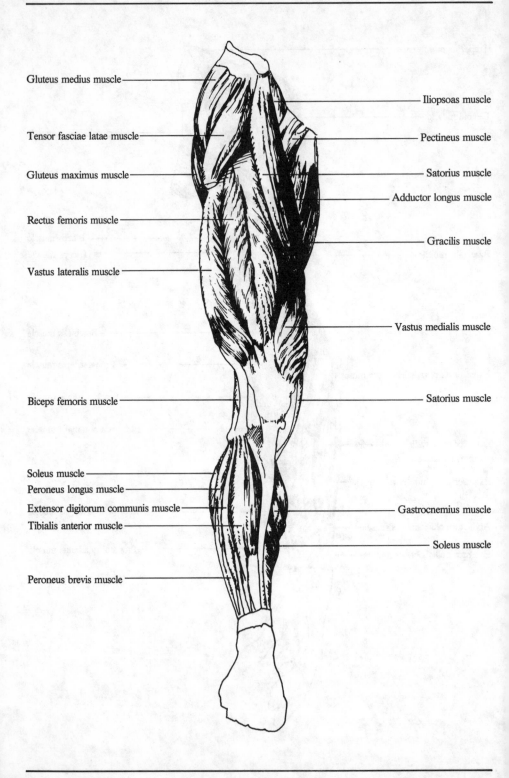

Gluteus medius muscle

Tensor fasciae latae muscle

Gluteus maximus muscle

Rectus femoris muscle

Vastus lateralis muscle

Biceps femoris muscle

Soleus muscle
Peroneus longus muscle
Extensor digitorum communis muscle
Tibialis anterior muscle

Peroneus brevis muscle

Iliopsoas muscle

Pectineus muscle

Satorius muscle

Adductor longus muscle

Gracilis muscle

Vastus medialis muscle

Satorius muscle

Gastrocnemius muscle

Soleus muscle

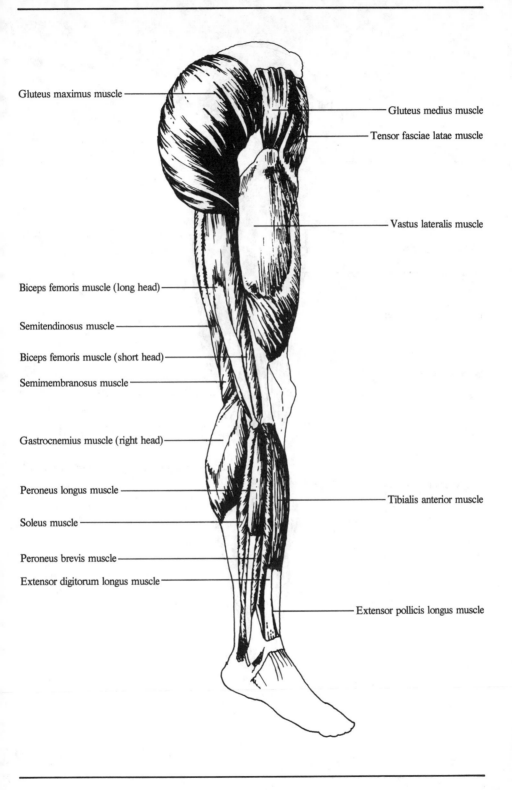

Gluteus maximus muscle

Gluteus medius muscle

Tensor fasciae latae muscle

Vastus lateralis muscle

Biceps femoris muscle (long head)

Semitendinosus muscle

Biceps femoris muscle (short head)

Semimembranosus muscle

Gastrocnemius muscle (right head)

Peroneus longus muscle

Soleus muscle

Peroneus brevis muscle

Extensor digitorum longus muscle

Tibialis anterior muscle

Extensor pollicis longus muscle

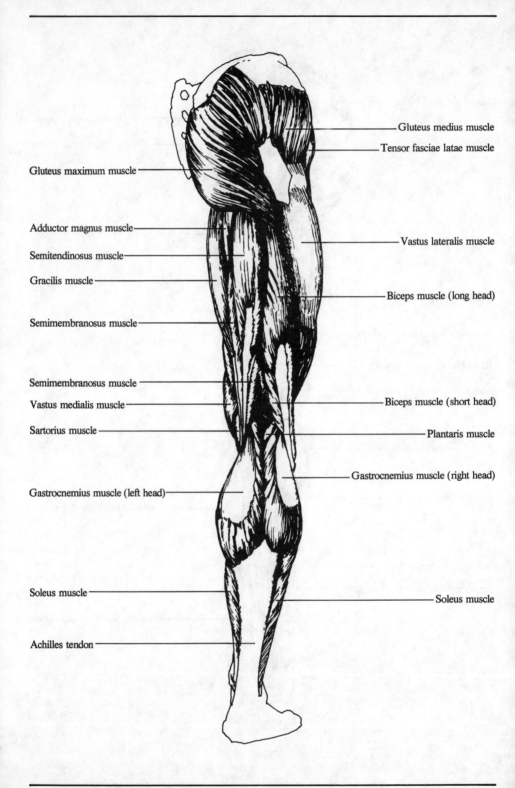

Gluteus medius muscle

Tensor fasciae latae muscle

Gluteus maximum muscle

Adductor magnus muscle

Semitendinosus muscle

Gracilis muscle

Vastus lateralis muscle

Semimembranosus muscle

Biceps muscle (long head)

Semimembranosus muscle

Vastus medialis muscle

Sartorius muscle

Biceps muscle (short head)

Plantaris muscle

Gastrocnemius muscle (right head)

Gastrocnemius muscle (left head)

Soleus muscle

Soleus muscle

Achilles tendon

PART I. FUNDAMENTALS OF KINEMATICS AND DYNAMICS

IA. Physics, Body Kinematics and Dynamics in General

This chapter discusses the relatively small collection of physical principles responsible for the tens of thousands of body techniques utilized in the martial arts, including karate. A few karate techniques will be used to specifically illustrate all these principles, but it will be stressed that the application to other body disciplines are quite general. The next Chapter IB, explains all the basic karate techniques using these principles.

IA-1. Notation

First, we must establish an clear and specific vocabulary to define our techniques. Techniques to be executed and, where added description is necessary, transitions between techniques will be set off by square brackets [...]. The description of each technique will follow the order in which power is generated: Start from the base, usually the floor, and progress to each body area and, if necessary, include its relationship to connecting body areas. As you will see, there are so many possible moves and connections that this precise vocabulary is necessary.

For example, [front-stance (R) counter-punch solar plexus] translates to front-stance, "R" means right leg forward; "counter" means punch with same hand in the furthest (left) leg from the target; target is the solar plexus of your opponent, and the direction of power is assumed to be in front of you. In this book the target "solar plexus" will often be used interchangeably with "stomach." The use of "counter" may seem odd. It originates from the fact that typically one blocks with the arm closest to the approaching attack, naturally the arm on the side of the closest leg, and then "counters" with a technique from the other side of the body. Note that each sub-part of a technique referring to one entity or movement is connected by hyphens.

[Side-stance (W) reverse-rotation (N) knife-hand-block (R)] translates to: side-stance facing west (W), an arbitrary reference direction; reverse-rotation method of hip power to the north (N) relative to the side-stance from a perspective looking down to the floor from a height above the action; knife-hand-block with the right hand (R). So, we have relative directions of the compass (N,S,E,W) pointing out from your body, and also labels of parts of your body relative to your midline (R,L). Usually, these directions refer to the most typical use of the technique: [Front-stance (S)] translates to front-stance facing south; [front-stance punch (E)] translates to punch in the direction the front-stance is facing, which is east. The target area is not specified and so is your

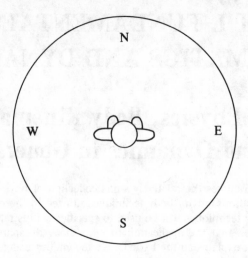

choice. Sometimes the line of power from your hip center to the target is not along the typical facing position of the stance. In these cases more notation is usually added, sometimes at the risk of being redundant just to help the novice. [Side-stance (N) hook-punch (L,E)] translates to: from side-stance facing north, hook-punch with the left hand to the east (towards the right side of your body). In circular techniques, where the power line from hip to center is not straight, the initial and final points will usually determine the notation.

Unless otherwise stated, techniques are assumed to start from [front-stance (L)] facing front, sometimes labeled north (N). Kicks are assumed to be performed with the leg furthest from the target. Many techniques have several variations, and unless otherwise specified, it is assumed that the main variation discussed in this book is the one being referred to. For example, the main [knife-hand-block] is defined here with the elbow bent 90 degrees, and the wrist kept straight. [Knife-hand-block bent-wrist] would refer to the variation performed with the elbow straight and wrist bent 90 degrees.

Between techniques, a comma "[...],[...]" represents a space where the body comes back to a relatively uncompressed or unstretched state. A hyphen "[...]-[...]" represents a connection between techniques without any such intervening space. An ampersand "[...]&[...]" represents techniques performed simultaneously. A slash "[...]/[...]" or "[.../...]" represents either (not both) technique may be performed. An asterisk "[*...]" represents a technique "[...]" performed slowly. An exclamation point "[!...]" represents a kiai during "[...]". "A:" represents the initial attack side in an exercise, and "D:" represents the initial defense side. A string of techniques or a sub-combination may be set off by additional brackets: "[A: [...],[...]-[...]]&[D: [...],[...]-[...]]". This translates to a three-step sparring sequence in which both the attacker and defender are moving to the rhythm of "one", and then "two-three". Occasionally, reference must be made to specific techniques or connections that are to be done simultaneously by opponents. These reference-points will be marked by (#n), where n = 1,2,3...,depending on how many such reference points are required in the interaction.

The above notation is sufficient to discuss all techniques, and still flexible enough to permit the individual instructor and students to add or change techniques by simply writing more information into "[...]" spaces. If square brackets are not available on your typewriter, I suggest using "%(...)%".

IA-2. Forces and Stance

Karate techniques are designed to deliver large impact forces to their targets. To attain such forces, the attacking body must possess great momentum. The usual way to attain such momentum is to apply a force to a large mass and quickly accelerate it to an extremely high velocity. Momentum is defined as this mass multiplied by its velocity. The force required is approximately equal to the final momentum available, inversely weighted by the overall time interval. When this force is applied to a small target area, tremendous pressure -- force divided by target area -- is created capable of producing shock and sometimes breakage.

At first glance, it may seem that the human body is not well designed to accomplish this feat -- that the attainment of large mass and the attainment of great speed are mutually exclusive: On one hand, large masses can be created by tensing and connecting the heavy parts of the body, making it a rigid extension of the floor. But in this state the body is too stiff to produce any speed. On the other hand, great speeds may be attained by the arm or leg when propelled from the supported torso and stance, much as a stone is shot from a sling. However, this fast moving limb does not have a large mass on impact.

To achieve both mass and speed, the arm or leg which has been just previously shot from the torso and stance can be tensed just before impact, then reconnected to the torso, and thus to the large mass of the lower body which is connected to the ground by the stance leg(s). However, while this technique attaches a large mass to the limb, it eventually slows the limb down. There is a compromise possible such that a large momentum (mass x velocity) is available upon impact with the target. Depending on the target and the strategy, various proportions of mass and velocity may be selected to contribute to produce large momentum. This is the essence of "focus".

Exercise IA-1

The source of power needed to generate techniques in karate can be traced to proper use of the legs in a stance. Stance is the term used to describe the legs when they are in tension and connected to each other by the continuation of this tension through the center of the body. The two basic types of stance are outside-tension stance and inside-tension stance.

The stance provides the forces and torques to move the torso, which in turn spins off the arms and legs. A torque, which is produced by two or more forces acting in opposite directions at each end of a lever, is necessary to rotate the body about a given point in space. In contrast, only a single force is necessary to cause the motion of the body along a given straight line in space. The forces from the stance are important to accelerate the limbs. Upon impact from a blow, the stance also provides rigid support to help establish a large grounded mass behind the technique.

The proper stance is also necessary to acquire a smooth quick start for most techniques. For example, in front stance, initiate a quick start forwards: Release the front leg of the stance, allowing the back leg which is already driving forward to push the body directly and smoothly. If the front leg switches from pushing to pulling, instead of merely releasing, additional force is generated to drive you forwards.

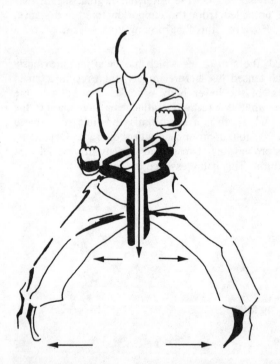

Figure IA-1a. The side-stance is an outside-tension stance.

Figure IA-1b. The hour-glass-stance is an inside-tension stance.

Exercise IA-2

The general structure or form of any stance can be analyzed using three basic concepts: balance, power, and mobility. Maximum balance is obtained when the center of gravity is low. However, if a stance is too low, it is extremely difficult to use the inside thigh muscles to move the body, and power and mobility are lost. For example, to take the proper long distance for [front-stance], begin by placing your left foot about two and one half shoulder-widths ahead of your right foot.

Figure IA-2. The proper front-stance has a long distance between the heels of about two and a half shoulders' width.

Exercise IA-3

To determine the width of the [front-stance], along a line perpendicular to the one in which you are facing, consider balance: Too narrow a stance makes it difficult to maintain balance, and too wide a stance is not stable against recoil upon impact. A good estimate of the proper distance is one shoulder-width between your feet.

To best direct power from your back leg, turn your right ankle in towards center as much as possible (30 to 45 degrees), but still keep the entire sole touching the floor. The side edge of your front (left) ankle should be parallel to the line of motion -- toes turned slightly in. If your ankle is turned in too much, mobility is lost. If it is turned out too much, your leg muscles are stretched out and cannot develop maximum power.

Your left knee should be positioned directly over your large toe. If your knee is not bent enough, the reaction force from a simple punch will push your hips back. If your knee is bent too much, the sharp angle will become a weak point because tensing the outside muscles of a sharply bent limb produces a weak corner. Consider building a bridge shaped like a "V" or an "A". The sharp corner would break under a stress that could be comfortably accepted by a smooth arch. If your knee is bent correctly, muscles can be tensed to construct a smooth arch of tension on the inside of your legs. Forces travel faster in a medium with strong elastic forces between its building blocks. Therefore the forces in a proper stance will travel more efficiently through the strong arch across inside of the knee rather than traveling across the top of the relatively more relaxed musculature of the top of the knee. This protects the knee joint from stress and also allows larger muscle regions across the whole leg to be integrated into a single stronger entity.

Figure IA-3. The proper front-stance has a lateral distance of about one shoulders' width.

Exercise IA-4

This principle of providing smooth arches of tensed muscle to direct the flow of forces is utilized over the entire body. Many disciplines, for example aikido, stress the principle of smooth arches of tension as a necessary component towards developing a proper flow of ki (chi), life-force, through the body and into the target or environment. More important than the outer appearance of the form are inner tensions under the arm across the abdomen, and across the insides of the thighs to produce an unbroken connection of smooth arches.

Your hip center must be properly tensed to transmit the forces and tensions between the legs, through the torso, and out to the external limbs. The iliopsoas (short double muscle high on the thigh and hip), internal oblique (middle layer of abdominal muscle on the sides), transversus abdominal (innermost layer of abdominal region), and sartorius (long narrow muscle connected to the spine that winds downward and inward across the thigh) muscles must be tensed so that the inside thigh muscles can bridge forces through the hip center to the torso and limbs.

Figure IA-4. The [counter-punch] illustrates how a technique is constructed as a system of smoothly connected arches.

Exercise IA-5

Breathing and proper hip feeling are fundamental to all techniques. For example, stand in [natural-stance], your feet about a shoulder-width apart, body relaxed. To avoid tensing to form just an outer shell of hard muscle, put one hand on your rectus abdominis (outermost layer of abdominal muscle that runs from the pubis to the ribs) and the other on your gluteus maximus (buttocks) and tuck up the lower trunk by flexing the iliopsoas, keeping the outside layers of muscle rather relaxed. This movement necessitates the tensing of the inner muscles and facilitates pushing up the diaphragm, expelling air. Slowly tense the most inner muscles that you can feel, starting at a point projected midway along a line between your navel and your tailbone, then gradually allow this compression to expand radially outwards until the outer rectus abdominis and gluteus maximus muscles are also tensed. As you tense, the diaphragm is slowly pushed up expelling air. Near the end of this "low" breathing, the chest and ribs then compress, effecting a "high" breathing, finally forcing out all your air. When you release, the diaphragm lowers and air is automatically taken in. At the peak compression you should notice a solid feeling of connection across the legs and through the torso.

Now do the same exercise at a faster tempo until the air is forcefully expelled as the hips quickly tense. Simultaneously tense the ribs to effect "high" rapid breathing. This rapid expulsion of air together with the associated noise that usually accompanies this movement is called a kiai (life-breath). The kiai is not practiced to frighten unworthy opponents! It is used to aid the body to focus energy, just as a grunt enables you to lift a heavy weight.

Hold the hands overhead and continue the radial compression described above to include the back, sides, neck, legs, arms, feet, and fists. Make the fist by folding all the knuckles into a ball, capped by the thumb placed under the first two fingers, and keeping a straight line from the elbow through the lowest knuckle of the second finger. A [fist], in karate terminology, is this complete body feeling centered in the hip. All true body techniques in the martial arts require this complete unity, centered in the hips.

When kneeling, or on one knee, the stance principles remain the same. The concept of stance can even be applied when lying on the floor. Then both hands grabbing the floor and one thigh can be used to produce power across the hips, for example, to execute a kick with the other leg.

As briefly mentioned before, a single technique typically requires at least two stances, one at its beginning and one at its end focus. The before-stance at the beginning is used to initiate large accelerations to gather up speed for the technique. The after-stance at focus is used to connect mass to this fast moving technique. If the body hardly moves, then the before-stance and after-stance may appear to be the same. But, more obviously, if a large shifting motion takes place, the before-stance and after-stance can be quite different.

A rather subtle point is: What happens between before-stance and after-stance? Actually, this is the most important part of the technique, during which most of the work takes place while power is generated. The art is to somehow smoothly change the body kinematics, to go from stressing acceleration, to stressing mass connection, to maximize the momentum at focus. In Section IIA-1, exercises will be given to better understand this transition, using as an example the counter-punch. In general, each technique in the martial arts requires some special feelings to get this most efficient transition. Any small change of a joint angle and distance relative to neighboring joints changes the strengths, weaknesses, and maximal use of muscles across that joint. Although only the few basic physical principles discussed in this chapter are required to analyze and to help correct all techniques, each technique must be carefully and regularly practiced many times to achieve excellence.

The discipline of "kinesiology" is an empirical science which typically studies the movements of accomplished athletes in specialized activities to better understand these transitions. However, most of the successes of kinesiology have been in its hindsight. Each discipline must be separately studied, but their similarities can best be understood by studying their common kinematics.

Figure IA-5a. Just after inhaling, the body is in a relaxed position.

Figure IA-5b. Just after exhaling, the hips are tucked under and the abdomen is tensed.

Figure IA-5c. A [fist] is not an isolated hand technique, but rather a complete body technique.

IA-3. Producing Momentum
with the Hips

Although the body typically works as an integral unit, it is convenient and helpful to consider how the stance acts on the central torso to further shape the power that is eventually directed to the target. We refer to the kinematics of this relay station as "hip power."

a. BODY VIBRATION. The first mode of hip power to be considered is the production of vibrations in the torso.

Exercise IA-6

This method is illustrated by [side-stance punch]. The tension across the legs and abdomen in the side-stance is similar to that in a taut guitar string. One hand, the pulling hand, pulls back and "plucks" this tension to produce a body vibration. It requires many years of training to teach the large muscle groups of the body to spontaneously and correctly initiate powerful movements. Without this training, everyone's natural immature instinct is to rock the head and shoulders that produce forces to then react on these large torso muscles to begin their movements. It is more efficient, and does not break balance and power, to use the pulling hand to initiate these large movements. Once the large muscles of the body are moving together, it is easy to use them to throw the other hand, [punch], off the hip to the target. Instead of using vibration energy to produce sound, as in the case of the guitar, the hip vibration-energy is directed into building the momentum of the punching arm.

Figure IA-6. [Side-stance punch] is created by vibrating the tension across the hips and stance with the pulling hand.

Exercise IA-7

The trajectory, or path of the punch must allow the arm to be most receptive to the transfer of power from the body. Place your right fist, palm up, at the soft spot between the bottom of the rib-cage and the top of the hip bone. This position keeps the bicep muscles relaxed and the elbow close to the hip. Hold your left arm straight out in front of you so that your fist is level with your solar plexus. Then move your right fist forward while pulling your left fist back to its hip position. As the punching elbow clears the hip, a little resistance can be felt from the arm muscles, so it is most natural to allow the forearm to twist, giving a shearing motion to the punch. Throughout the punch, minimize tension on the outside of the arm and over the shoulder to maintain a smooth arch under the arm -- tensing the latissimus dorsi and serratus anterior muscles (along the ribs) -- to transfer the forces. Again, it is important in all movements to synchronize physical movement and breathing. Proper coordination between hundreds of muscles is best learned by synchronizing them with the beginning and end of a breath.

b. ROTATION. Another movement that takes advantage of stance forces is hip rotation. A more complete discussion of rotation will be postponed until striking techniques.

Figure IA-7. Just as the [punch] clears the hip, it begins a shearing rotation.

Exercise IA-8

The front-stance can be used to deliver [counter-punch], a punch from the same side as the back leg. Retaining the tension across the knees, start in front-stance with right fist on hip, left fist forward. Using circular forces around each leg, turn the hip about its center. Be careful not to break the primary tension across the knees.

The pulling hand helps initiate this technique by pulling back on the hip, jolting the large torso muscles and helping them to coordinate the rotation used to throw off the punching hand. The pulling hand aids the punching by setting up the correct reaction forces to initiate the body dynamics. If you imagine a pole placed horizontally across the torso, you can easily visualize how the pulling hand sets the body in motion to throw off the punching hand. A force on one end of a pole causes a rotation about the center of the pole.

The punching trajectory is the same as described before. The pulling-hand helps the hip to rotate. While only one point of contact with the ground is necessary to move the body in a straight line, it is necessary to have two points of contact to perform a rotation in order that equal and opposite forces can be applied to turn the body about its center.

You should appreciate the fact that you do not produce something from nothing. You must work to put power into your techniques. You know how tiring it can be to push a car or to just push against a wall. Although your arm or leg weighs much less than a car, if you expend the same maximum effort at each moment during your punch as if pushing such a heavy object, then that effort will be used to accelerate your limb to the maximum speed possible.

c. REVERSE ROTATION. Another power method is called reverse rotation.

Figure IA-8a. The beginning rotation of the hip starts to spin off the [counter-punch].

Figure IA-8b. The middle of the hip rotation continues to spin off the [counter-punch].

Figure IA-8c. The end of the hip rotation coincides with the end of the [counter-punch].

Exercise IA-9

An imaginary stick can be used to explain this new method of transferring momentum. In the previous discussion, an imaginary stick was placed across the body to generate the muscular action necessary to drive the opposite arm. Now imagine the stick placed along your arm, and allow your armpit to develop a "swivel-joint" feeling. When your body now rotates in one direction, your arm will rotate in the opposite direction. Actually, this power method is not really new. When walking, each arm moves in the opposite direction to its nearest hip. By doing this, the reaction force of your rotating hips is taken up by your arms, permitting your spine to stay straight and relatively free of strain. In a reverse-rotation technique a strong hip motion causes the arm to move with great power.

d. SHIFTING. A fourth hip power method is [shifting], whereby the torso and center of mass is itself accelerated to give additional speed to the arm or leg technique. Lateral shifting is more sophisticated and is discussed in the next section.

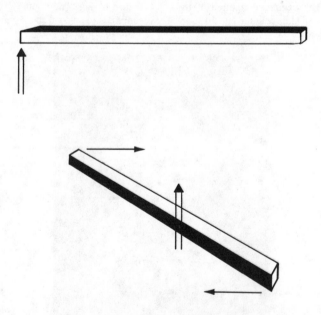

Figure IA-9. [Reverse-rotation] can be understood as the reaction felt at one end of a stick from an action perpendicular to the other end.

Exercise IA-10

To understand how stances effect forward shifting, step from [front-stance] one full step ahead to a new [front-stance] according to the following sequence: Opposing forces should already exist between your legs. Your front leg, which now controls the entire motion, changes its direction of force from pushing away from the body to pulling with the inside and back thigh muscles. The effect of this movement on shifting is twofold. Releasing the outward force allows the pushing force from the back leg to drive the body forward. In addition, this motion of the body is aided by the pulling scissor motion of the front pulling leg. As your legs cross and the direction of force again changes, your left leg now becomes the back leg for the next front-stance. The left leg now pushes away from the body, driving it continuously forward, until the right leg brakes the forward motion by coming to rest. Note that the full step-in motion, typical of any large body motion, involves the use of many forces in the body, each of which are usually only singularly emphasized in a single stance. This step-in motion requires the use of both inside-tension and outside-tension stances, discussed in Section IB-1. Individual techniques are therefore best appreciated as important training devices, which must be respected and mastered, but not worshiped as limitations to the way the body can creatively move.

Figure IA-10. At the very start of [step-in] the back leg is pushing the body, and the front leg has just started pulling.

Exercise IA-11

In a [step-in punch], the [punch] must be coordinated with the body motion of shifting. Begin in [front-stance (L)], right fist on hip, left fist forward. Then step in to a new [front-stance punching]. The proper technique requires that the arm and body achieve maximum momentum together upon impact. (Momentum = mass x velocity.) Ideally, your punch should begin when your legs start to move. Every body part should smoothly accelerate and reach a maximum focus at the instant you are achieving a new front stance. At first, you will probably not be able to move your legs quickly enough to allow the punch to begin until after your legs have crossed, but with practice, the punch may be started sooner and sooner as the leg movements become more coordinated. Your pulling hand may help the start by creating the desired reaction force in the hip. Use the punch as a self-competitive device to drive yourself to move faster by beginning the punch sooner than you might think possible. Try to have the arms and legs coordinate to achieve focus together. You might move faster than you thought you could!

The feeling in the body during these accelerated motions (of the arm with respect to the body and of the body with respect to the ground) is similar to that felt when pushing against a wall while in front-stance. The force flowing from the back leg through the hip and arm is met by an equal and opposite reaction force exerted by the wall. Upon releasing the arms, a reaction force from the front leg is required to prevent any forward motion. Release your front leg to direct a flow of force continually from your back leg through your arms, then release your arms to direct a flow of force through the front leg, and keep rapidly alternating this flow of force to better understand its origins.

Figure IA-11a. The beginning of [step-in punch (R)].

Figure IA-11b. The middle of [step-in punch (R)].

Figure IA-11c. The end of [step-in punch (R)].

Exercise IA-12

When accelerating an arm or a leg, similar forces are necessary to overcome the inertial mass. Although the forces have different purposes in static and in dynamic situations, the feeling in the muscles is essentially the same. For example, when doing a step-in punch, the body should propel the arm and legs with much the same continuous driving feeling as experienced when pushing against the wall. The dynamic reaction forces exerted on the body by the propelled punch are countered by the force exerted by the legs on the body in the opposite direction. Thus the forces necessary to step-in-punch are ultimately dependent on the proper use of stance for both the arm and body motions.

e. JUMPING AND SLIDING. Once the mechanics of basic shifting are mastered, it is also straightforward to integrate arm and leg technique with jumping and sliding (at least one foot always touching the ground). The important new feature is to adjust these techniques to the new body timing required to have complete body focus at the target.

Figure IA-12. The feeling of pushing against a wall is a useful analogy to the feeling of continually accelerating the body.

IA-4. Torques and Angular Momentum

a. TORQUE AND INERTIA. It is now time to study the rotation movements in more detail. Many analogies can be made between the dynamics of linear and curvilinear movements. To create linear motion, you applied forces or reaction forces to accelerate the masses of your arms, legs, and body, producing momentum at the target. The momentum you produced continued along its line of motion until it was stopped by forces from another body or by internal forces such as friction. You were also able to transfer momentum from the body to the arms and legs to produce fast-moving projectiles.

In equation form:

F (force) $=$ m (mass) x a (acceleration);

v (velocity) imparted to m by F is

$v = a$ x t (time).

At any time, t,

P (momentum) $=$ m x v.

The inertia, I, of a body of mass with respect to a point a distance r away, about which it is rotating is equal to

$I = m$ x r x r.

The angular momentum, A, possessed by this rotating mass, is equal to

$A = m$ x v x r,

where v is the tangential velocity of the mass around the center. The angular velocity, w, is expressed as

$w = v/r$.

Torque is necessary to accelerate and rotate inertia to produce angular momentum (a spinning motion). Angular momentum tends to continue its circular motion until stopped by other torques.

Exercise IA-13

The concept of inertia can be readily understood in body language by performing the following exercise. Assume a front-stance, keeping arms outstretched with underarms tensed so that the arms move rigidly with the hips. First, rotate the hips and arms with maximum torque across the hips to cause the hips to rotate. Practice rotating the hips and arms several times.

Second, bend the arms at the elbow, and do the same hip motion. Then do the movement a third time, clasping your elbows with your hands. Now do the first exercise once more, and notice how much harder it is to get up the same angular speed with the first exercise as compared to the third. In each case the mass moved was the same, but the inertia was different.

Many practitioners tend to confuse how strong a technique "feels" with the actual power in the technique that can be directed into the target. With linear techniques, one's intuition is a fairly sound guide. If you work harder to produce a technique, that technique will probably be faster and stronger. However, with curved or rotating techniques, one must be more analytic. You will work harder to move your arms, legs, or body in relatively large circles, but the power available for focus will actually be less than that produced by keeping the smallest rotations about the center of movement as you strive to approach the target at the desired angle.

Figure IA-13. You can appreciate how inertia is different from mass by swinging your outstretched arms.

Exercise IA-14

b. STRIKE-LOCK AND STRIKE-SNAP TECHNIQUES. You can transfer this rotation motion -- angular momentum -- to other body parts. This is analogous to transferring linear momentum from the body to the arm in a step-in-punch. From one back-stance, rotate 180 degrees to another back-stance, swinging the arm and focusing the back of the fist on an imaginary target. To get maximum speed, sweep the elbow across the body, bending it as it crosses through the center, then letting it whip out to the target. This motion is most efficient because the inertia is minimized in the middle of the motion by bending the elbow. The distance from the center of rotation is almost zero, which allows the greatest speed to be built up for a given torque from the legs and hips. Be sure to tense the small group of muscles under the arm and on the sides of the ribs to lock the arm, preventing a rocking motion at focus. This technique feels like a whip: A large mass with your torso as the handle of the whip starts a rotation motion. This angular momentum continues to ripple down the whip to the end, whereupon the small mass, your fist as the knot of the whip, is accelerated to very high speeds. This motion is called a strike-lock technique because, upon focus, the arm locks to the body, attaching body mass to the arm. Whereas thrusting techniques approach their target as arrows, striking techniques approach their target as swinging sticks.

Figure IA-14a. To begin a [strike-lock] bring
the elbow across the center of the body.

Figure IA-14b. Just before the forearm
begins its stage of the [strike-lock] the elbow,
hip and back leg are lined up into the target.

Figure IA-14c. At the focus of [strike-lock
bottom-fist] the forearm swings into the target.

Exercise IA-15

STRIKE-SNAP. Another striking technique is the strike-snap motion, so-called because of a snap-back, or recoil, movement. For variety, practice this technique with a different method of hip power: Attempt [reverse-rotation down-block] by stepping back with the right leg from natural stance (feet close together) to front-stance. Next, allow your left elbow to go straight to a target at face level, rather than down to a block. Your hips rotate in one direction; your arm rotates in the opposite direction. As your hips complete their 45 degree rotation, lock the underarm of your striking arm to your body but keep your elbow joint rather flexible, maintaining a "spongy" feeling. The dynamics of this "spongy" feeling will be explained later in the section on Energy. The spinning motion given to your arm thus "leaks out" and is transferred to your forearm, which spins out very quickly from the upper-arm again, similar to the action of a released stretched spring. After focus, the snap-back returns the fist towards the center of the body.

The transfer of angular momentum may be algebraically described as follows: Let the inertias of the body (rotating about the center), the arm (rotating about the shoulder joint), and the forearm (rotating about the elbow joint), be denoted by I (body), I (arm), and I (forearm), respectively. Let the angular velocity of the body, the arm, and the forearm be denoted by w (body), w (arm), and w (forearm), respectively. Then conservation of angular momentum A at each stage, transferred down to the arm by a system of levers, implies that:
A = I (body) x w (body) = I (arm) x w (arm).
A = I (arm) x w (arm) = I (forearm) x w (forearm).
Some algebra shows that
w (forearm) = (I (body)/I (forearm)) x w (body)
Since I (body) is greater than I (forearm), we see that the angular velocity of the forearm becomes much greater than the angular velocity of the body (neglecting friction at the joints).

Thus you can transform the large inertia of your body into a large angular speed of your forearm. This is quite similar to using the principles of linear momentum applied to many thrusting techniques; for example, a moving body mass can be used to develop quicker punches.

Figure IA-15. The [strike-snap] is accomplished by allowing the forearm to snap back from the end of [strike-lock].

Exercise IA-16

Striking techniques take advantage of the small inertia of the striking limb. Aside from strategy (choice of technique, timing, and distance), a given technique can most efficiently transfer momentum when the target and the projectile have equal masses. Try the three cases of a moving marble hitting another marble at rest of mass equal to, less than, and greater than the moving marble. It is assumed in this simple discussion that no heat is generated in the collisions. The marbles are assumed to be completely ideal and elastic. Only in the third case, which is familiar to all those who have played marbles, billiards, or pool, can the momentum of one marble be completely transferred to the other. With a given momentum available, the various thrusting and striking techniques give a rather wide range of masses to use against various targets (face, body, and so forth) in order to accomplish maximum transfer of momentum.

Strike-lock and strike-snap techniques can be applied at many joints of the body. To continue this study, another technique, [front-snap-kick], will be discussed.

This kick can be understood on two levels. On one level, the concepts of forces and reaction forces are used to analyze each limb motion as it contributes to the total technique. On the other level, concepts of linear momentum, angular momentum, and energy, discussed in the next section, describe the total process more abstractly, but also easily lead to generalization. An understanding of the second level will enable you to learn all the snap-kicks almost simultaneously, so that you won't need to spend weeks imitating and memorizing a different body feeling for each technique.

BEFORE M2 IS AT REST	$M1 > M2$	$M1 < M2$	$M1 = M2$
	M1 → ○M2	M1○ → (M2)	(M1) → (M2)
AFTER	(M1) → M2○ →	M1○ ← (M2) →	(M1) (M2) →

Figure IA-16. A complete transfer of energy between colliding elastic bodies is only possible if they both have the same mass.

Exercise IA-17

The fundamentals of [front-snap-kick] are best learned with one hand placed against the wall for balance. The kick is usually delivered with the ball of the foot, although sometimes the toes are turned down to make a "fist." Although your ankle is rigid upon impact, keep it somewhat flexible during the kick to continuously direct a straight line from your heel through the ball of the foot directly into the target. From [front-stance (L)], move the back leg to kick by changing your front leg from pushing out to pulling in, as in the beginning of the step-in-punch. If not done properly, the shoulders will jerk back involuntarily to cause the reaction force necessary to move the leg. This motion breaks balance and prevents the body from compressing when focusing during impact.

In executing the [snap-kick], you must rotate the line connecting the solar plexus to the knee about the solar plexus as center. Minimize inertia to obtain maximum speed -- that is, as your knee progresses toward the target, bend it sharply in order to keep most of your leg as close to the center of rotation for as much of the kicking trajectory as possible. This occurs quite naturally as your knee accelerates toward the target: Your calf is rotated up to the back of your thigh because of a reaction force that is described in the use of the reverse-rotation techniques.

Create tensions inside curves that run along the inside and top of your thigh and the abdominal walls to help lock your front leg to your body just when the line from the center of your hip through your knee is finally pointing to the target. Your back leg directs force through this imaginary line, feeling like the back leg of front-stance. If the knee is now kept flexible, the force that stops the leg motion whips out the foot by effecting another reverse-rotation force. Your leg automatically springs back as your knee assumes the "spongy" feeling similar to that used in the arm strike-snap techniques. If the muscular expansion and contraction of all the body muscles follows the rhythm of this flow, this kick becomes a very strong technique.

In thrusting techniques, the body is rigid and compressed upon focus. In striking techniques, the body first stretches into the target. The hip and abdominal regions then compress with the snap-back of the technique. In all techniques some method of total body connection is necessary.

A more general way of looking at the snap-kick technique is to observe that a torque from the original front-stance produces a spinning movement using the line from the solar plexus to the knee as the radius of the circular motion. This angular momentum is then transferred to the lower leg when the stance (standing) leg acting at the solar plexus exerts a counter-torque to still the body. This way of viewing the kick is essential to develop a total body feeling of the technique. The former analytic description, in terms of reverse rotation and rotation forces at each joint, is most helpful to analyze and correct your techniques.

c. APPLICATION TO BODY MOVEMENTS. Some of the principles described above can be utilized to effect dynamic rotational and sidewards body motion. In the next exercises, start from a front-stance, although any other stance would also work. In both rotational and sidewards motion, the lateral components of the forces between the legs are used.

Figure IA-17. The [front-snap-kick] drives the knee to the target much the same as the elbow is driven to its target in [strike-snap].

Exercise IA-18

Circle-shifting is accomplished by rotating the body, using the front leg as a pivot. The pivot leg changes its lateral component of force from outward to inward, which enables both legs to forcibly rotate the body. As your back leg rotates around, allow the inside thigh muscles that are pulling on the inside of your front leg to connect and pull along the inside thigh muscles of your back leg. This will pull your legs together during the rotation, minimizing their inertia and maximally accelerating the turn.

Figure IA-18a. At the beginning of [circle-shift] laterally pull the back leg towards the hip-center.

Figure IA-18b. In the middle of [circle-shift] the body is rotating while all the mass of the body is close to the spine line.

Figure IA-18c. At the end of [circle-shift] the body has rotated to a new angle.

Exercise IA-19

Side-shifting is accomplished by releasing the horizontal force on the back leg to allow a sidewards motion to begin. Bring your back leg through the center of the body, and drive it back along a 90 degree axis, simultaneously rotating and pushing your front leg outward along the floor to the side. It now becomes the front leg of a front-stance at the new 90 degree angle.

Figure IA-19a. At the beginning of [side-shift] the back leg is pulled towards the hip-center while the front leg pushes laterally outward.

Figure IA-19b. In the middle of [side-shift] the body is rotating and shifting to the side of the attack.

Figure IA-19c. At the end of [side-shift] the body has rotated to a new angle.

Exercise IA-20

You can experience the sensation of complete body rotation in tumbling, which a few methods of falling will illustrate. In every fall, the spine is kept smoothly curved by tucking in the pelvis, tucking in the chin, and maintaining an even tension along the curved spine. The purpose is to convert some of the energy gained in the fall into harmless rolling, rotational energy.

In previous examples, the torso made turning motions similar to motions in the falls, but the movement was accomplished by using the legs to torque the torso. By utilizing gravity to help perform these falls, you can better realize a more total three-dimensionality to all techniques. Learning to fall is, of course, essential before seriously practicing leg sweeps (variations of crescent kicking) and throws discussed in Chapter IB.

Figure IA-20. During a [fall] keep your pelvis and chin tucked in.

IA-5. Body Expansion & Compression

Energy, another physical principle commonly applied to karate techniques, is composed of three forms:

Energy (total) = Energy (motion) + Energy (compression) + Energy (heat).

Energy (motion) = (momentum) x (momentum)/(2 x mass).

Energy (heat) is caused by friction in the muscles, biochemical processes, and so forth; it cannot be practically retrieved. Energy (compression) from compressed muscles can be reused to produce the beginning of another technique much the same as motion can be obtained from a compressed spring or sponge-ball.

Exercise IA-21

This principle is primarily responsible for the smooth flow between the two techniques in the simple exercise: [counter-punch]-[step-in counter-punch]. The expansion from the first counter-punch not only helps the torso prepare for the next compression (second counter-punch), but also puts extra tension across the stance which is used to quickly step forward by initially pulling in with the front leg. The use of this muscular compression and expansion across the arms, legs, and torso gives rise to the "spongy" feeling necessary to do the strike-snap techniques discussed in the previous section.

Body rhythm is aided by knowing and using physical laws of force, energy, and motion. The momentum and energy created for one technique can serve the next technique as well.

Figure IA-21a. The focusing of one [counter-punch] can be used as preparation for another technique, by using the stance and torso as a large spring.

Figure IA-21b. The spring from the first [counter-punch] can be used to gain a moment's advantage to continue the attack.

Figure IA-21c. A [step-in counter-punch] from [counter-punch] is effected by using the spring energy from the latter technique to help start the former.

Exercise IA-22

In order to smoothly integrate individual techniques into combinations as well as to perfect each technique, body expansion and compression must be learned. A simple exercise taken from the kata (stylized sequence of movements), Heian #1, illustrates the possibilities of such technique-to technique connections: Try [[step-in-punch],[step-in-punch]-[step-in-punch]]. After the first punch, wait until the body springs back to the neutral state, or state of even body tone, before triggering the start of the second punch. Although the momentum of the body stops after the first punch, the inside muscular expansion and compression continues. After the second punch however, continue momentum and also use the compression of that punch to trigger the start of the third punch. Between these last two punches both the outside and inside movements of the body are uninterrupted.

IB. Basic Body Kinematics of Karate Techniques

IB-1. Stances

Section IA-2 has already given the purpose and method of stance, the use of the legs and hips to develop strong torques and forces from the floor to act on the torso. In this chapter, all the major stances used in karate techniques will be presented.

Exercise IB-1

a. NATURAL-STANCE. Keep your hips tucked under. Stand with your feet about a shoulder's width apart, body relaxed. Test your readiness to move by trying a few quick starts forward, back, and to each side. Natural stance is the feeling just before moving.

The next series of stances is composed of outside-tension stances, wherein the legs create tension across the hips and abdomen by pushing apart. Remember to start each stance with your hips tucked under to make it possible for maximum forces in your legs to be transmitted to your torso.

Figure IB-1. [Natural-stance] is the feeling just before moving.

Exercise IB-2

b. FRONT-STANCE. Place the left foot about two and a half shoulder's width ahead of your right foot. Keep the lateral distance across your feet the same as it was in natural stance, about a shoulder's width apart. Keep the side edge of the front (left) foot straight ahead, and the side edge of the back (right) foot turned in as much as possible, between 30 and 45 degrees. Be sure to keep the front knee bent over the large toe, but keep the tensions following along the inside of the leg. With proper training, your back knee may be slightly bent, enabling the thigh and calf muscles to tense to direct a straight line of force from the center of the hip to the center of your arch. If any joint becomes too rigidly locked, forces cannot flow smoothly across it, and the force transmitted across the neighboring limbs actually becomes weaker, even though a small group of muscles in the vicinity of the joint may be more strongly tensed in the locked position. However, at first, you may have to settle for a straight back leg until you can pick up the proper muscle feeling. Under no conditions allow any joint to become hyperextended. If your joints have a natural propensity to hyperextend, then try harder to more quickly learn the correct muscle feeling to protect your joints from incorrect stresses that might otherwise be encountered.

A blend of [natural-stance] and [front-stance] gives rise to [free-stance]. This stance has the outward appearance of [front-stance], but the softer inside feeling of [natural-stance]. The elbows and knees feel as if they are gently pressing in and being pushed out by a large balloon in front of the hips.

Figure IB-2a. [Front-stance].

Figure IB-2b. [Free-stance] is a blend of [front-stance] and [natural-stance].

Exercise IB-3

c. SIDE-STANCE. The front-stance is easiest for beginners to learn because it faces forward and because the back leg directly pushes the hip forward via the reaction force from the ground. This is a familiar feeling when walking or running. The side-stance is somewhat more subtle.

The distance between the feet is the same in the side-stance as in the front-stance. The tension across the legs and hips allows the body to deliver power to either side. In the side-stance, the knee and lower leg (actually the smooth curve inside and across the knee) push out, and the floor pushes back. When doing side-stance, be sure to keep the outsides of the feet parallel and the hips tucked in. An outward circular tension exerted around each thigh will keep the back and inside of each leg tense and drive the hips forwards.

Figure IB-3. [Side-stance].

Exercise IB-4

d. BACK-STANCE. This stance is essentially half side-stance and half front-stance. Your back leg is used somewhat as in side-stance, though it is bent even more. Your front foot is twisted out at an angle so that its outside edge is parallel to the line between your heels. The knee of the front leg is only slightly bent; any locked joint prevents an even tension from flowing across it. Except for the opposite direction of the ankle, the front leg of the back-stance resembles the back leg of the front-stance in its direct method of pushing into the floor. The heels are along the same line to prevent the production of torques on the hip that would break balance.

Figure IB-4. [Back-stance] is a blend of [side-stance] and [front-stance].

Exercise IB-5

e. ANGULAR-SIDE-STANCE. Place the feet in side-stance at an angle of 30 to 45 degrees to the direction both your hips are facing. This stance is capable of making and focusing power in all directions, although it is not as strong to the front as front-stance, or as strong to the side as side-stance. A smooth band of tension circling the legs should be realized.

The next series of stances are inside-tension stances, wherein the legs create tension across the lips and abdomen by pulling together.

Figure IB-5. [Angular-side-stance] is essentially a [side-stance] at an angle to the line of power.

Exercise IB-6

f. HALF-MOON-STANCE. This is the inside-tension analogue of the outside-tension angular-side-stance. The distance between the feet is the same as in angular-side-stance. The back ankle is turned in almost forward, and each knee is pulled towards the inside of the opposite ankle. More correctly, smooth curves of tension pull towards each other, from the soles of the feet up to the imaginary extensions of the legs meeting at the solar plexus. Be sure the hips are tucked under to lock these two tensions together.

Figure IB-6. [Half-moon-stance] is an inside-tension stance at the same angle and distance between the heels as [angular-side-stance].

Exercise IB-7

g. HOUR-GLASS-STANCE. When sparring at close distances, often the feet must be close together. At distances between the legs approaching a shoulder's width, the angle between the thighs in front-stance becomes too small to produce an effective horizontal component of force to push against the ground to derive strong body power. The hour-glass-stance solves this problem. This stance is essentially the same as the half-moon-stance, except that the large toe of the back leg is on a line that passes under the center of the body and through the heel of the front leg. The relevant angle that determines components of force on the floor is measured by intersecting lines along the lower legs that pass from the heels through the knees. This angle is much steeper than the angle between the thighs in a front-stance with the same distance between the feet.

Figure IB-7. [Hour-glass-stance] is an inside-tension stance that is more useful than [front-stance] when the feet are close together.

Exercise IB-8

h. CAT-STANCE. This is the inside-tension analogue of the close-distance outside-tension back-stance. It is produced by pulling the front leg of the hour-glass-stance over until the front heel is just in front of the big toe of the back leg. The front heel is raised and the thighs are pinched, crossing the front knee over the back knee. As in all the inside-tension stances, the tensions in the legs should be extended up to the solar plexus.

Figure IB-8. [Cat-stance] is an inside-tension stance that is more useful than [back-stance] when the feet are close together.

IB-2. Punching

Although the concept of punching seems straightforward, keep in mind, and in practice, that only the proper use of stance and hip movement discussed in Sections IA-2-3 will generate power for the punch. In fact, you will do better to start realizing that the punch, like all karate techniques, is really a body technique. Think of the arm as a convenient extension of the body that increases your range, and also is a convenient limb that can translate the larger-mass body momentum into a lighter-mass faster technique.

Exercise IB-9

a. COUNTER-PUNCH. Exercise IA-4 in Section IA-3 contains a description of how the arm is typically connected to the body driving a punch. (Occasionally the ball-and-swivel feeling of reverse-rotation hip motion is used.) Try exercise IA-5 to study the most common punch, [counter-punch].

Figure IB-9. [Counter-punch].

Exercise IB-10

b. STEP-IN-PUNCH. Exercise IA-11 describes [step-in-punch]. A somewhat subtle point is the proper use of the pulling-hand. In [counter-punch] the feeling under both arms is a "direct-connection," an elastic feeling, not so rigid that the arm can't be accelerated off the body, and not so loose that the arm does not quickly respond to the motion of the body. In [step-in-punch] the feeling under the punching arm is also direct-connection, but the feeling under the pulling arm is reverse-rotation. Here, the action of the pulling arm tends to reverse-rotate the hip opposite to the punching hand, thereby locking both hips square into the punch. Note that this is the opposite muscle order usually used by reverse-rotation: Usually the reverse-rotating body acts on the hand to produce a technique.

c. BASIC PUNCH VARIATIONS. There are several variations of the basic [punch] or [counter-punch] which vary only in their reach or method of body power.

Figure IB-10. The pulling-hand at the focus of [step-in punch] applies a [reverse-rotation] force to its hip.

Exercise IB-11

When the target is closer to the body than the fully extended arm, the punch is simply focussed in the same position it would have on the trajectory of the fully extended punch. When the elbow stops about two fists past the hip, the [vertical-punch] is performed with the fist in a vertical position, thumb-side up. When the elbow stops next to the hip, the [close-punch] is performed with the palm-side of fist facing up. The wrist turns outwards on focus to help lock the punch to the body. Admittedly a poor choice of nomenclature, the [short-punch] is actually a fully extended punch done with the arm on the same side as the front leg. The "short" title refers to the shorter distance from the hip to target when compared to the counter-punch. The [u-punch] is a simultaneous punch to the face and close-punch to the solar plexus. Sometimes the spine bends and the head also attacks like the middle prong of a trident. The [double-punch] is composed of two simultaneous punches keeping the posture vertical.

    d. TRAJECTORY VARIATIONS IN PUNCHING. There are also three variations in punching that change the trajectory, or path through space, that the arm follows. These are usually still classified as punches.

Figure IB-11a. [Vertical-punch] is focused with the elbow about two fists' distance from the hip.

Figure IB-11b. [Close-punch] is focused with the elbow touching the hip.

Exercise IB-12

ROUND-PUNCH. This punch takes a curved trajectory towards its target. This is aided by pulling around the hip with the pulling hand, setting up some lateral reaction force on the punching hand. The punching forearm also twists before the elbow clears the hip. This sets up tensions that permit the body to throw out the arm in a curve away from the line connecting the hip center and the target. However, twist the forearm as you near the target, using the compression of the stance and abdomen to pull the arm back into the line connecting the hip and the target. This punch is also used effectively as a simultaneous block under an opponent's attacking arm.

Figure IB-12. [Round-punch] is often used as a combination of [punch] and [up-block].

Exercise IB-13

RISING-PUNCH. This punch begins its course as a punch to the groin level, but swings up in a vertical circle, usually attacking under the chin. This is accomplished by first tensing the sides of the abdomen along a vertical channel, allowing the compression from the low punch to drive the punching hand upwards. Then the abdomen is compressed horizontally as well to solidly lock the punching arm to the body upon focus. These imagined "channels" help to correctly lock the arm to the body along its trajectory.

Figure IB-13a. [Rising-punch] starts a vertical swing from an attack towards the groin.

Figure IB-13b. [Rising-punch] ends as an attack under the opponent's chin.

Exercise IB-14

HOOK-PUNCH. This punch takes a horizontal 90 degree swing across the body to the target. Just as the elbow of a would-be normal punch clears the hip, the forearm twists inwards, and the punch travels parallel to the chest. This punch is effected by first tensing horizontally across the abdomen, creating a horizontal channel for the arm. On impact, the vertical compression locks the arm to the body.

It is especially important when doing [hook-punch], [rising-punch] or [round-punch] that a strong tension is maintained under the arm-body connection, and that any tensions along the outside of the arm-shoulder line are minimized.

e. ADDITIONAL HAND TECHNIQUES FOR PUNCHING. Using the principles developed so far, several hand techniques may be affixed to the punching arm to accommodate various targets and strategies.

Figure IB-14. [Hook-punch] is useful at short distances attacking towards the side.

Exercise IB-15

The [one-knuckle-fist] is made by protruding the middle finger's second knuckle before the fist is clenched as the striking weapon. The [fore-knuckle-fist] is made by protruding the forefinger and placing the thumb almost inside under the second knuckle before clenching the fist. The [ridge-knuckle-fist] is made like the fore-knuckle-fist, except that all the second knuckles are protruded.

Various open-hand techniques are also used for punching. The [palm-heel] is made with the wrist bent back 90 degrees and the second knuckles of all the fingers closed tightly in a vertical position. The [spear-hand] is made by keeping the fore-finger straight, curving the next two fingers to make the tops of all these fingers level, and tensing the hand uniformly from the little finger side and from the thumb side. The [two-finger-spear-hand] is made by slightly curving the first two fingers and clenching the others. Sometimes the finger next to the index finger is only half-bent to give additional support to the index finger. The [one-finger-spear-hand] is made by slightly curving the first finger and half-bending the others for support. The [bear-claw] is a palm thrust with fingers spread apart and slightly curled forwards. All open hand punching techniques are not performed with a shearing component at focus, as this would tend to break the fingers.

Figure IB-15a. [One-knuckle-fist].

Figure IB-15b. [Ridge-knuckle-fist].

Figure IB-15c. [Spear-hand].

Figure IB-15d. [Two-finger-spear-hand].

IB-3. Blocking

Hip rotation is extremely useful for [attack-blocks], which are designed to break the opponent's rhythm and balance as a prelude to a counter-attack. Use the arm and hip closest to the opponent. When facing in a given direction, you can effectively direct power perpendicular to an attack over an extremely wide angular region.

Another method of blocking, which is smoother but requires better timing, is [sweep-blocking], in which the attacking momentum of the opponent is controlled along a line tangential to the attack. The blocking hand glides along the attacking limb, exerting a gradual sideways force that smoothly deflects the attack. This method of control is used to a great extent in judo and aikido.

As will be discussed below, [attack-blocks] can be turned into [attack-sweep-blocks] which have some sweeping component to them, and vice versa. Other categories of blocking are mentioned below.

The attack-blocks as well as the attacks follow principles of natural body movements: One group of muscles should not impede another group's functions. An important application of these principles is: When the blocking (or punching) hand is close to your body, the palm naturally faces toward you, and when the hand is extended, the palm naturally faces away from you. These positions minimize arm tensions that could interfere with the flow of power coming from the legs and hips.

Exercise IB-16

a. UP-BLOCKING. Begin [up-block] as a would-be punch along a vertical line in front of the center of your body. When your wrist reaches the height of your head, twist out your forearm to form a smooth curve extending under your arm. The position of your fist should be about two fist-widths from the top and front of the head. Keep tensions under the arm, and avoid stiff shoulders that can disconnect the block from its source of speed and mass, the body.

Figure IB-16. [Up-block].

Exercise IB-17

You can also use the extra twist of the forearm at the end of the up-block to turn your wrist up for a smoother deflection of the attack. The timing of this twist with the focus of the block allows you a continuum of blocking methods ranging from a heavy attack-block that is perpendicular to the attacking line of motion, to a smoother sweep-block that rolls along the attacking line of motion. This variation can also be applied to the following two blocks.

Figure IB-17a. [Sweep-up-block] makes initial contact sooner than an [attack-block].

Figure IB-17b. The final position of [sweep-up-block] is the same as [up-block].

Exercise IB-18

b. ROUND BLOCK. Start the round-block with your arm bent out to the side at shoulder height and the fist by the ear. A smooth rotation down and toward the center of the body ends with your palm facing inward at shoulder height with the elbow bent at a 90 degree angle about two fists' width from the body. This block is also called [outside-round-block] because it starts from the outside of the body.

Figure IB-18. [Outside-round-block].

Exercise IB-19

INSIDE-ROUND-BLOCK. This variation of [round-block] starts from under the arm of the pulling hand, and sweeps out laterally to block. Whereas [outside-round-block] makes contact with the small finger side of the forearm, [inside-round-block] makes contact with the thumb side of the forearm.

Figure IB-19. [Inside-round-block].

Exercise IB-20

c. DOWN-BLOCK. The third basic attack-block is the down-block. Begin with your fist next to the opposite ear, palm facing in. Swing your arm down across the front of your body and twist your forearm out just as your arm becomes nearly straight. At the focus of the block, your palm should be facing down and the line of your arm should be parallel with the front thigh as it would be in a front-stance.

Figure IB-20. [Down-block].

Exercise IB-21

OUTSIDE-DOWN-BLOCK. The above [down-block] travels from the inside of body towards the outside of the body, and could more specifically be called [inside-down-block]. The [outside-down-block] is performed by swinging the straight arm from the outside of the body across the front of the hips.

All the blocks may utilize the power methods [reverse-rotation], [vibration], [shifting], as well as [direct-rotation].

In the [direct-rotation down-block], the pulling hand is pulled in the direction opposite to the hip movement to act as a brake, focusing the hip rotation by pulling against its direct rotation coupling. In [reverse-rotation down-block], where the blocking hand and hip move in opposite directions, the pulling hand directly helps to rotate the hips with the direct underarm muscular connection.

Figure IB-21. [Outside-down-block].

Exercise IB-22

d. KNIFE-HAND-BLOCK. This technique begins as an [inside-down-block], but with the opened blocking hand facing the opposite ear. However, the block ends with a twist of the forearm, elbow locked at 90 degrees and a couple of fists distance away from the blocking hip. This is more precisely an [inside-bent-elbow-knife-hand-down-block stomach].

For close-distance sparring, the open hand reacts more quickly than the fist. The back-stance is also useful for close-distance sparring because after blocking it is relatively easy to spring into front-stance with a counter-punch.

Figure   IB-22.   [Inside-knife-hand-block stomach].

Exercise IB-23

BENT-WRIST-KNIFE-HAND-BLOCK. This variation of [knife-hand-block] starts out as [inside-round-block] and ends with a straight elbow and bent wrist. Fingers should be bent at the first and second joints, and the palm should be vertical.

In all hand techniques, be careful of the position of the elbow relative to its hip. If the elbow goes just a bit behind the hip, then the back muscles naturally fold in towards the spine. The elbow must stay in front of the hip in order to maximally flare out the back and latissimus dorsi muscles to help lock the arm to the torso.

Figure IB-23. [Inside-bent-wrist-knife-hand-block face].

Exercise IB-24

e. CATEGORIES OF BLOCKS. As they relate to their influence on targets, there are several other main categories of blocks. [Attack-blocks] have momentum perpendicular to that of their targets. [Sweep-blocks] ride along tangentially to the momentum of their targets, with a slighter pressure applied for a longer contact time than with attack-blocks, which serves to deflect the attack. [Attack-sweep] blocks are attack-blocks with some sweeping component, as discussed for the up-block. [Hook-blocks] are [attack-inside-blocks] performed with a straight joint (usually wrist or elbow) that immediately bends on contact to twist and break the opponent's balance. [Round-punch-block] is a [round-punch] that is used to simultaneously block and punch.

[Augmented-blocks] use the other hand to support the blocking hand. Usually the fist by the inside-elbow, or the open hand pressed by the wrist of the blocking hand is used. [X-blocks] are made by crossing the hands just below the wrists. Typical x-blocks are [up-x-block], [down-x-block]. [Two-hand-sweep-defense] is typically used against a kick, with one hand doing the actual blocking, and the other hand crossed over to prevent the kick from riding up the blocking hand to attack your face or body. Double-blocks use two simultaneous blocks: [Double-up-block] and [double-outside/inside-round-block] are examples.

Figure IB-24a. [Augmented-inside-round-block].

Figure IB-24b. [Two-hand-sweep-defense].

Exercise IB-25

f. ADDITIONAL HAND TECHNIQUES FOR BLOCKING. Using the principles previously described, several hand techniques may be affixed to the blocking arm to accommodate various targets and strategies.

[Back-fist] is usually used against fleshy target areas, and [bottom-fist] (little finger side of fist) may be used anywhere. There is a little more variety available with the open hand: [Knife-hand] is the little finger side of the spear-hand. [Ridge-hand] is the thumb side of the same hand, but the thumb is pressed down to the bottom of the little finger, exposing the bottom edge of the fore-finger. [Back-hand] and [open-palm] may be used as well. [Tiger-paw], usually used as part of a sweep-block, grabs just as contact is made. The thumb and fingers are curved to a half circle and tension is maintained inside until contact, when the hand automatically closes.

Figure IB-25a. [Ridge-hand-sweep-defense face]&[counter-punch face].

Figure IB-25b. [Tiger-paw].

Exercise IB-26

Four main regions of the wrist are also used for blocks: [Chicken-head] is made by touching the thumb to the little finger, and using the thumb-side edge of the bent wrist. [Tortoise-head] is made by touching the thumb to the index finger, and using the flat part of the bent wrist. The [palm-heel] is made by bending the wrist back 90 degrees, and using the bottom of the palm. [Ox-jaw] is made by bending up the thumb-side edge of the wrist, using the little finger side of the wrist-palm corner.

Figure IB-26a. [Chicken-head block].

Figure IB-26b. [Tortoise-head block].

Figure IB-26c. [Palm-heel block].

Figure IB-26d. [Ox-jaw block].

IB-4. Striking

Section IA-4 has discussed the physical principles behind striking techniques. Now we will examine the basic variations of [striking].

a. STRIKE-LOCK. These techniques swing into their target, and focus with the body rigidly connected, similar to thrusting techniques such as [punch]. Note that the [attack-blocks] can also be considered as strike-lock techniques.

Exercise IB-27

The most basic [strike-lock] is [bottom-fist-strike-lock]. The arm motion is essentially a [down-block], but to a vital target instead of to an opponent's attacking limb. With the hand under the opposite arm, the elbow leads to the target, with the forearm as close to the center of upper-arm rotation as possible. The elbow then locks to the torso, and the forearm swings out to strike the target with the bottom-fist (small-finger side of the fist).

Figure IB-27. [Bottom-fist-strike-lock ribs].

Exercise IB-28

Another common variation is [back-fist-strike-lock] which unfolds just as the [bottom-fist-strike-lock]. However, just near the target, the forearm twists outwards, striking the target with the back of the knuckles of the first two fingers.

Figure IB-28. [Back-fist-strike-lock neck].

Exercise IB-29

ELBOW-STRIKES. The elbow can directly drive to the target. Even the novice will appreciate the strong mass connection available at this close distance to the target. [Counter-elbow-strike face] drives up to chin, with the palm facing the ear as the pivot point for the technique. [Counter-elbow-strike stomach] drives to the solar-plexus, with the palm facing down near to your stomach as the pivot point for the technique. [Inside-elbow-strike] starts from inside the body, and swings out to the target with the palm facing down swinging across the chest into the target.

b. STRIKE-SNAP. These techniques unfold just like the [strike-lock] techniques. However, on focus, instead of locking to the torso, the [strike-snap] limb snaps back from the target, depositing a faster-velocity quality of momentum into the target than the larger-mass quality of momentum afforded by the [strike-lock] techniques.

Figure IB-29a. [Counter-elbow-strike face].

Figure IB-29b. [Counter-elbow-strike stomach].

Figure IB-29c. [Inside-elbow-strike stomach].

Exercise IB-30

The [strike] limb may be the elbow, as in [bottom-fist-strike] or [back-fist-strike]. It may be the wrist, if the entire body behind the wrist becomes solid on focus, similar to the handle of a whip, and the momentum produced at that joint transfers to the fist. The [strike] limb may be at the shoulder if the entire arm swings to target, or the hip itself if the whole body swings into the target.

Note that all four basic hip movements described in Section IA-3 are available for striking techniques.

c. ADDITIONAL HAND TECHNIQUES FOR STRIKING. For completeness, other hand techniques used for striking are briefly discussed. These, of course, use the principles previously discussed.

Figure IB-30. Just after focus of [cat-stance strike-snap face].

Exercise IB-31

The techniques described in the Section IB-2e, Additional Hand Techniques For Punching, and those in Section IB-3f, Additional Hand Techniques for Blocking, can be used for striking. These include: [back-fist], [bottom-fist], [knife-hand], [ridge-hand], [back-hand], [chicken-head], [tortoise-head], [palm-head], and [ox-jaw]. The tip of the [spear-hand] may be used (carefully in practice!) to the eyes. The [rising-punch], using the back of the knuckles, can also be considered a striking technique. [Thumb-knuckle] is made by pressing the thumb against the second knuckle of the forefinger of the clenched fist. [Bear-claw] is made by bending all the fingers at the second knuckle. [Eagle-beak] is made by flexing the wrist and touching the tips of all fingers.

It is often very efficient to smoothly whip back and forth with the same hand, between [ox-jaw] and [chicken-head] or between [tortoise-head] and [palm-heel], to make useful [attack]-[block] or [double-attack/block] combinations.

Figure IB-31a. [Ox-jaw-strike-lock stomach].

Figure IB-31b. [Bear-claw-strike-lock face].

IB-5. Thrust-Kicking

[Thrust-kicks] are quite analogous to [punches]. All these techniques gather up speed from stance and hip movements, create speed in the attacking limbs, and, at the focus of the torso and attacking limb, connect and directly pierce into the target.

The basic [front-thrust-kick], [side-thrust-kick], and [back-thrust-kick], begin with one leg pulled up close to the center of the body while the hip motion is being controlled by the stance leg. In all kicks, curve the body as a lens focusing into the target. If your hands, head or shoulders fly wildly about, you are not developing power from [stance]. In general the abdomen pulls the leg through center, while simultaneously the stance leg drives the hip and kick to the target.

Exercise IB-32

a. FRONT-THRUST-KICK. To do this, first assume front-stance, left leg forward, with your hips tucked under. You might want to hold lightly on a wall or some other object with one hand for balance when you first practice kicks. Use your abdomen to pick up your kicking leg, above the knee of the other leg. If you don't clear your own knee, you may soon break your toes on your opponent's shin! Then drive your right leg to the target along the line from your knee through the ball of your foot, using force which comes from your stance (left) leg through your hip. Instead of the ball of the foot, sometimes the heel is used. Then bring your kicking leg back to the center of your body to allow a smooth transition to step into next stance. Use your abdominal muscles to control the kicking leg throughout its trajectory. This allows your leg muscles to be relaxed to be most receptive to momentum from your hip. As with the underarm connection in the punch, there should be an elastic-feeling connection between your leg and torso. The connection is minimal at first, allowing the leg to accelerate away from the hip and attain a high velocity. It becomes maximum at the focus as it unites the leg with the more massive torso, supported by the rigid stance leg. The stance leg upon focus is the same as the back leg of [front-stance].

Figure IB-32. [Front-thrust-kick stomach].

Exercise IB-33

b. SIDE-THRUST-KICK. To do [side-thrust-kick], drive the leg to target along the line from the knee through the side edge of your foot with the stance leg being used as in [side-stance] to drive the hips sideways. Remember to keep your hips tucked under just as in [front-kick].

The position of the ankle in kicks is very important, as it directly affects the angle of the thigh relative to the torso. The analogous problem with the hand relative to the torso is not as severe, although it is present. For example, in [front-thrust-kick], if the ankle turns inwards, the stance and abdominal muscles are no longer as strong to the front. Maximum strength from this ankle position is derived by swinging the leg around, keeping the side-edge of the foot parallel to the ground, to [side-thrust-kick] position. Similarly note that if the toes are turned upwards, power is lost to the side, and is restored only by swinging the leg around to [front-thrust-kick] position. The stance leg is like [side-stance].

Figure IB-33a. [Side-thrust-kick stomach].

Figure IB-33b. [Flying-side-thrust-kick].

Exercise IB-34

c. BACK-THRUST-KICK. Similar to the experiences described in the above paragraph, maximum power is obtained by having the foot as vertical as possible to the floor, heel pointing up. The line of power for this kick, as in the other [thrust-kicks] requires that the front-stance-leg is furthest from the target, and the hip-center in some middle region before the target. The hips must be tucked under in order to maximize power generated from the stance and abdomen, even though the back is somewhat curved towards the target. The stance leg is like the front leg of [front-stance].

Figure IB-34. [Back-thrust-kick groin].

Exercise IB-35

.d. STOMP-KICK. This essentially a [side-thrust-kick] performed directly down to a target, such as an opponent's instep or knee. There are two variations. [Close-stomp-kick] starts with the knee up to the center-line and then directly drives down at angle to the target. [Far-stomp-kick] starts with the knee coming up to the center-line, but then the lower-leg arches out over the target, as if extending into a long [side-stance]. Then the body and leg drop down onto the target.

Figure IB-35. [Stomp-kick knee].

IB-6. Swing-Kicking

Exercise IB-36

a. CRESCENT-KICK. Another basic kick that you can practice at this stage is [crescent-kick]. It utilizes hip-rotation to swing the sole of the back leg into the target. This [kick] can be used as a [block] or as an [attack].

Figure IB-36. [Crescent-kick block].

Exercise IB-37

b. SWEEP. The swinging motion used in [crescent-kick] can be applied to the bottom of the calf or ankle of the opponent. [Crescent-kick] and [sweep] as described above are obviously leg analogues of the arm [strike-lock] techniques using [direct-rotation]. They can also be performed with [reverse-rotation]. As the swinging leg nears the target, change the hip-joint feeling to the ball-and-swivel feeling of [reverse-rotation], and snap the hips back in the opposite direction upon focus. This imparts additional speed to the swinging leg, with some loss of mass connection. The [hook-sweep-kick] pulls the target towards you just as contact is made.

Figure IB-37. [Sweep ankle].

Exercise IB-38

c. WHEEL-KICK. The back of the heel is swung behind you, attacking the target. This kick can also be done with [direct-rotation] or [reverse-rotation].

Figure IB-38. [Wheel-kick face].

Exercise IB-39

d. KNEE-KICKS. The knee can be directly swung to the target. Although not as fast as the extended kicks, even the novice can appreciate a strong mass connection behind these close-distance techniques. [Front-knee-kick] drives directly forward. [Round-knee-kick] comes up and around, as if kicking over a table, but curving the torso into the target. [Side-knee-kick] drives directly sidewards into the target. At close distances, sometimes the toes are curled to a "fist" to protect them.

Figure IB-39a. [Front-knee-kick].

Figure IB-39b. [Round-knee-kick].

IB-7. Snap-kicking

Analogous to the arm [strike-snap] techniques, the leg can execute [snap-kick] techniques. The line from the solar plexus to the knee can rotate in three planes to produce [front-snap-kick], [round-snap-kick] and [side-snap-kick].

Exercise IB-40

a. FRONT-SNAP-KICK. This kick is described in detail in Section IA, Exercise IA-17. The knee drives forward as in [front-knee-kick], the body locks, and the bottom of the leg whips to the target and snaps back to center. The stance leg is like the back leg of [front-stance]. Sometimes the instep or toes curled to a "fist" are used, instead of the ball of the foot, to attack.

Figure IB-40a. Just before focus of [front-snap-kick].

Figure IB-40b. Focus of [front-snap-kick].

Figure IB-40c. Just after focus of [front-snap-kick].

Exercise IB-41

b. SIDE-SNAP-KICK. The same dynamic process can produce a [side-snap-kick] to attack a target to the side, using the outside edge of the foot near the heel. Be careful not to turn the toes and ankle out. If you do, your thigh muscles also will twist out. From the point of view of reverse-rotation forces, the bottom of your leg is scooped up towards the groin as your knee shoots out as it does in [side-knee-kick]. Your knee should drive out at an angle of about 45 degrees from the front of the body rather than to the center as in the [side-thrust-kick]. When your thigh locks, making it a rigid extension of the torso, the spinning motion originally generated in the torso and leg is transferred to the lower leg. The leg then whips back to center. The stance leg is like [side-stance].

Figure IB-41a. Focus of [side-snap-kick face].

Figure IB-41b. Just after focus of [side-snap-kick face].

Exercise IB-42

c. ROUND-SNAP-KICK. The [round-snap-kick] is done in the third plane (horizontal) of your three-dimensional space. The kicking leg essentially does the [front-snap-kick], but in the horizontal plane. Use your side muscles to help pick up the leg so that your heel, ball of your foot, knee, and hip are equal distances from the ground. Rotate your hip and knee 90 degrees, so that the bottom of your leg is driven to the back of the thigh. Lock your knee and hip along the line to the target as in [round-knee-kick] to spin off your lower leg. The stance leg is like [side-stance]. As with the other snap kicks, it is easy to step smoothly into the next stance and technique.

The [inside-round-snap-kick] starts as a [front-kick], but the hip-center curves the knee and drives the kick to the corner outside the same side as the kicking leg. The [round-front-snap-kick] is performed in the 45 degree plane, half-way between the planes of the front and round kicks.

[Back-snap-kick] is useful at close distances, to the groin of an opponent attacking your back. In [natural-stance], the abdomen and thigh lock and snap-up your lower leg.

Many of the kicks can be performed while jumping. Some of the most popular are the [flying-front-kick], [flying-side-thrust (or snap)-kick] (legs used alternately), and the [flying-front]&[side (snap or thrust)-kick] (legs also used alternately).

Figure IB-42a. Focus of [round-snap-kick stomach].

Figure IB-42b. Just after focus of [round-snap-kick stomach].

IB-8. Throws

[Throws] require smooth torquing motions and sometimes subtle joint-twisting techniques. One's opponent as well as one's self must be continually controlled during the rotation movements. It is most useful in karate to consider [throws] like [blocks]: They are themselves incomplete techniques, but are useful, and sometimes necessary, to set up your opponent for an [attack]. For this purpose, the general rule to follow is to use as little force as possible, tugging or pulling, during these preparatory techniques. [Attacks] are the techniques that require fully committed force.

To carry out this general rule, don't try to lift or push the center-of-mass of your opponent. Instead, learn to quickly sense a weak axis of balance, and then apply torques about the center-of-mass to almost effortlessly rotate your opponent to the floor. Eventually, in free-sparring you will learn to shift into positions that threaten such weak axes. Your opponent will lose rhythm and position as you threaten these axes, and even though you have not accomplished a full throw, you will already have gained an important strategic edge in the interaction.

Exercise IB-43

[Step-in] to the open side of your opponent thrusting your hips close to your opponent's. Spread your arms/legs across the widest area of the opponent to obtain the largest torques. Turn your whole body 180 degrees to a new [front-stance], bringing your arms and your opponent down with you. Keep your own posture erect. It is a tremendous waste of power to use your torques to control your torso if it is off-center.

Figure IB-43a. Position to [throw] opponent attacking with [punch].

Figure IB-43b. Position during [throw] of opponent who is [punching].

Figure IB-43c. Position after [throwing] punching attacker.

Exercise IB-44

[Step-in] past a [kick], spreading your arms across your opponent. Obviously you must train to get good timing. Continue to move to the outside corner of your opponent, circling more and more until your opponent falls.

Figure IB-44a. Position to [throw] opponent attacking with [front-thrust-kick].

Figure IB-44b. Position during [throw] of opponent who is [kicking].

Figure IB-44c. Position after [throwing] kicking attacker.

Exercise IB-45

You can directly [pull] your opponent off balance if you can set up a counter-force to torque the center-of-mass. If your opponent has not just committed weight to a given leg, you can apply a counter-force by pressing against it with a sweeping motion, while you simultaneously pull on his or her arm.

One must be sensitive to the subtleties of "dynamic balance." If you are already quickly shifting in some direction this can serve as a source of support for techniques, without stopping for [stance], just as a moving train rightfully commands respect in its direction of motion. However, if you are pushing in a direction, then many times your balance is weaker at large angles away from this direction. Similarly, while your opponent is committed to quickly shifting, you may attempt breaking balance or [throwing] at some large angle to his or her direction of motion.

Figure IB-45. [Pulling] an opponent off balance with the aid of a [sweep ankle].

IC. Attention Dynamics

IC-1. Description and Motivation

Karate is often defined as a discipline offering a method of "self-defense against surprise attack." If we start with this definition, we are soon led to investigate and practice skills that to the novice must seem quite far removed from the original purpose. This is fine, because it enables an enlightened instructor to open the minds of his or her students, letting them acknowledge other alternative purposes for sweating several hours a week.

Self-defense requires at least three important perceptual mechanisms, which I will call processes or attention archetypes. One process, which some popular magazines, television shows and movies would have you believe is the ultimate answer for self-defense, is to develop yourself into a living, breathing machine gun, ready to indiscriminately mow down any and all transgressors of your sovereign space-time domain. This process of self-defense requires "focused attention" because it involves the ability to focus yourself to a specific space-time point, which is the target of your trained technique.

Sole reliance on this process for self-defense can be fatal, especially against a trained opponent who can strategically maneuver you into initiating your attack, and then suddenly counter-attacking. Miyamoto Musashi, the famous seventeenth century swordsman, was a master of this counter-attack strategy. Most professional competitive athletes are also aware of the deficiency of the strategy of waiting for a chance to execute a single pre-planned attack.

Equally important for self-defense, especially against a surprise attack, is to minimize all possible surprises. This means you must also train yourself to be sensitive and aware of your external environment as it rhythmically changes with you from past to future. To form viable strategies in the present, you must also be sensitive to your internal environment, your imagination and intuition. This "global attention" requires sensing patterns of space and time as they unfold in your total environment. There is always some appropriate scale of space and time at which there is continuity appropriate to perceive such patterns.

It is probably obvious, even to the novice, that suddenly hurling yourself to the ground in a focused effort to perform push-ups is hardly an elegant response to a correctly, globally perceived situation of imminent danger. Indeed some appropriate synchrony and coordination is required between your focused and global attention mechanisms. When, and only when all these perceptual processes are correctly brought to bear in a self-defense situation, the phenomenon of "good timing" is achieved. This is the magic for which audiences the world over pay tremendous sums of money, to view the superstars of their favorite physical and artistic disciplines or sports.

To those familiar with current research in neurophysiology and psychology, these global and focal attention archetypes correspond to right-left brain hemispheric functioning, to yin-yang, to female-male archetypes, etc. The success of most time-tested physical disciplines which requires regular training of exact body techniques, almost to obsession as an end in themselves, is the following: Involvement with an opponent, or one's own internal rhythm in case of some meditations, is also practiced until the student suddenly realizes the result of good timing as the essence of the activity. When this happens, the implication, often only expressed at the subconscious level, is that previously sought-after elusive intuitions and patterned flows perceived by global attention, have been made part of a decision-making process. This is a rather indirect method of achieving the realization and experience of global attention, but it works with anyone who has the perseverance to pursue a body discipline.

This book presents a teaching and learning methodology that from the very beginning presents feedback on global attention, without sacrificing insistence on correct technique and strongly focussed attention. Indeed, both attention archetypes are required for all concrete and abstract purposes which require synchrony of one's self with a complex, multifold task.

At every opportunity, all training exercises are to be studied as rigorous interactions involving decisions among techniques and strategies. The exercises present just enough complexity that the proper use of global attention makes the decision-making task easier, than by flitting back and forth between isolated perceptions and responses. The exercises are also just simple enough that stark feedback is readily available to highlight errors in body and attentional techniques.

A few exercises are presented in this chapter to serve as supplementary material to the courses given in PART II. These are useful to dramatically demonstrate the true existence of these attention archetypes, as well as to offer additional training to hone your perceptual abilities.

Figure IC-1. As described in Exercise IC-13,
two attackers face a single defender.

IC-2. Focal and Global

Attention Exercises

In karate, hip-centeredness is essential to develop strong body techniques as well as to facilitate correct mental activity. You should strive to become aware that your hips, especially as centered about a point midway on the diagonal line that connects the naval to the tailbone, comprise your motor center. Accordingly, as you become more proficient, you will find that your body acquires a "will" of its own, and you won't need to rely on much conscious activity to support its actions. This frees your mind to engage in strategy.

Exercise IC-1

To help separate some of the variables involved, [step-in punch] in a straight line towards an opponent who is steadily drifting away, moving from side to side. Keep your eyes fixed on the opponent so that your visual attention is occupied, and try to retain a sense of intense concentration on the most centered feeling in your hips. This exercise will make you aware that attention can be divided between you and your opponent.

Exercise IC-2

Reaction to your concentration to a point is an "all or nothing" matter. You can do a simple exercise to get immediate feedback on whether the process is present. Have your partner count sharply, each count a command to [punch] while you execute the proper technique. When you are punching, imagine that the sound coming from the voice into your ear can take two neurological paths: One path goes to the brain to tell you that a sound has been received; the other path triggers a body reflex to start the technique. If the exercise is done correctly, you will find yourself moving at the same time you become aware of the sound, not afterwards. Especially if you are a beginner, you will find that you perform the technique more smoothly and dynamically than you did previously -- that, indeed, the reaction feels more natural and instinctual.

Exercise IC-3

Another simple exercise is the visual counterpart of Exercise IC-2. Two people face each other in front-stance, same leg forward, in position to [counter-punch] in parallel lines to each other's opposite side. Person A counts, and it is prearranged that between two to four heartbeats after this count, Person B [counter-punches] Person A; at that time, Person A attempts to [counter-punch] Person B. It is often possible for both people to be counter-punching at the same time. If done correctly, Person A perceives Person B's motion simultaneously as he or she feels his or her own punch for reasons that are similar to the ones given in the auditory exercise above.

In any physical activity it is important to develop a sense of diffuse patterned attention, or an awareness in which complex movements are perceived as whole units. This sense of awareness is essential to attain a mastery of rhythm and timing. The next series of exercises serves to develop such an awareness.

Exercise IC-4

The first exercise is designed to develop a holistic sense of body rhythm. The best time to begin a technique depends on the demands of the situation. However, there are two optimal states from which the body is best prepared to move. One state, called the neutral, or natural, state is a state of body tone with a readiness to move in any direction. The major muscle groups are neither fully stretched nor compressed, but are prepared to expand or contract, depending on the need. Techniques connected by this state are referred to here as [...],[...]. The other state originates from a state of maximal compression or expansion, typically caused by the completion of a previous technique. Techniques connected by this state are referred to here as [...]-[...].

For example, from a natural-stance, [step-in front-stance punch]-[body-vibration counter-punch]. If you have achieved enough power and speed using the methods described so far, you cannot perform the second punch as a simple sequential response to the stimulus of compressed lower-abdominal and hip muscles. It takes a finite amount of time for messages to go back and forth to the brain before the arms can begin to execute the punch. It is too difficult to have one major somatic feeling be the stimulus to immediately trigger another major somatic feeling, and yet follow the pattern of compression/expansion. (This is not the case in the auditory-somatic and visual-somatic concentration exercise above.) By the time that you realize that the second punch should begin, the hips are no longer in a maximum state of compression, and the timing for the punch is ruined. When this occurs, an empty, hollow feeling is experienced under the arm of the punching hand because the arm is not being driven from the expansion following the first punch. Rather than guessing when to start the second punch, it is more educational to treat the two punches as one body rhythm of compression-expansion-compression. This is the major body feeling experienced by the torso and stance. Now retain a sense of the total rhythm and attempt to synchronize the actual movements with this rhythm. After a few trials, a patterned sense of body rhythm is realized, and both punches will be driven by power emanating from the motor center.

Exercise IC-5

Try incorporating the above sense of patterning into the combination: [front-snap-kick]-[step-into punch].

The following exercise is designed to teach auditory awareness. If there are multiple stimuli demanding different responses, it is not best to flit back and forth to be ready for the possible alternatives. If you are completely aware of your environment, the alternatives are known well enough, and you can assimilate them into one pattern which admits variations to trigger the required response. Consider a set of four such variations, each variation done to two counts.

Exercise IC-6

Begin in front stance, left foot forward. A first count -- e.g. "one" -- signals you to bring the back leg up to center (feet close). A second command -- e.g. "front" -- serves as a stimulus to a specific technique with the right hand:
"Front" -- continue to [step-in-punch (N)]
"Back" -- [step-back counter-punch (N)]
"Left" -- step back to the right side and [counter-punch (NW)]
"Right" -- step to the right side and [back-fist strike-snap (NE)]
Learn these techniques first by becoming able to respond to "front", for example, as a sound before becoming aware of "front" as a meaningful word (Exercise IIC-2). Conscious awareness of the word as an intellectual command should not trigger the technique. Now react correctly as your partner first counts "one", and then randomly commands one of the above four techniques. Your best reactions occur when treating all four possibilities as one pattern.

Exercise IC-7

Another auditory-pattern exercise is to react to the command "punch" or "kick". Have a partner give you either the command "punch" or "kick" as he or she chooses, alternating or repeating them in succession, so that you do not know which one is coming. It is best to give about three successive commands, each one triggering a successive technique: [punch]/[kick],[punch]/[kick],[punch]/[kick]. Best reactions are obtained by having the hip-center react to the command as if it were a variation of the single pattern comprising both possible commands. Interpret the command "punch" or "kick" by allowing the power to travel from the hip-center through your leg or arm, respectively. If instead of centering this power, your attention flits back and forth between an arm and leg, your body will not be maximally primed to do the required technique.

Exercise IC-8

An exercise that requires responses to visual patterns begins with both sides facing each other, each with the right leg forward, in front-stance. One side, by agreement, starts the exercise by executing [step-in punch (L) face]. The other side [steps-back up-blocks (L)]. Then one possibility allows either side to take a chance and [counter-punch (R) face/stomach]. If one side succeeds, the exercise is over. (If both sides attack at the same time, it is not a draw; both sides obviously lose!) Another possibility is having one side [block (L)] the other's attack to face or stomach, and then, if successful, to [counter-attack (R)] and win. These alternatives drive the opponents to heightened states of awareness.

Exercise IC-9

This visual-pattern exercise requires five people who have all practiced the first form, Heian #1. (This form is given in Section IC-3.) Four opponents face the center defender. Each of the five follows the tempo of the kata, the center person reacting to the other opponents by appropriately [blocking] or [attacking]. Each attacker must attack or block according to the theme and tempo of the form, but may [punch face/stomach], or even [front-kick stomach], when it is his or her turn to attack. Although this exercise requires a balance of somatic-centeredness and visual-pattern attention, all members should concern themselves primarily with moving to the rhythm and tempo of the form.

Exercise IC-10

While you [step-in-punch] to a point in space, [step-back], and then [step-in punch] to the same point in space, your opponent moves along your left side. Although you keep your eyes straight ahead, your peripheral visual sense remains occupied with the motion of your opponent. You retain a sense of your first target, selected by the first [punch], by projecting your proprioceptive sense (awareness of limb and internal organ positions) to feel contact with the target point. This point in space is touched with the second [punch], using a feeling similar to that when touching your hands behind the back. This exercise establishes the feeling of simultaneous and parallel, visual and somatic activity.

Exercise IC-11

In a three-step sparring exercise, the attacker [steps-in attacks] three times while the defender [steps-back block] each attack, [counter-punching] after the last block only. Each side keeps visual awareness of the opponent and somatic concentration to the focus of his or her own techniques. If the timing (synchronization) is off, either concentration or awareness is also off. This exercise coordinates visual and somatic awareness towards the same activity.

Exercise IC-12

In another exercise, called "enforced meditation," three or more people face each other for an unspecified length of time of 1 to 3 minutes, preset on a timer. Each person tries to maintain visual awareness over a wide area encompassing all opponents, synchronized with a centered feeling in the hip. When the timer rings, each person [punches] towards the opponent with the weakest attention(s). This exercise requires a harmony between visual and somatic activities geared to a specific purpose.

Exercise IC-13

In one variation, two attackers face a center defender at the NW and NE positions with the defender facing N. One other person behind (S) the defender gives the attackers the signal to [punch]. Again, the best response from the defender is achieved if both attackers are integrated into one rhythm, and variations of this rhythm excite the appropriate reaction. Each time the signaler commands an attack, the defender must block and [counter-punch]/[counter-kick], then be ready for the next attack if the signaler signals twice. The defender must keep awareness of both opponents, yet execute consecutive concentrated [blocks] and [counter-attacks] each time.

Exercise IC-14

In another variation, attackers are placed behind the line-of-sight of the defender, for example at the SW and SE positions. An attacker, upon a signal from the signaler, makes a noise to alert the defender, [stamp] or [counter-punch], then [step-into counter-punch].

In still another variation, attackers are placed in front and back. This requires visual and auditory awareness synchronized with somatic focused attention.

IC-3. Kata and Combinations

As stated before, global attention involves internal as well as external patterns. Internal patterns are essential for forming strategies to deal with the external patterns of the opponent. Practicing sharp responses to internal patterns can sharpen responses to external patterns and vice versa.

In karate, techniques can be put together in groups and patterns. You can build from words (individual techniques) to phrases (defense-attack sequences) to sentences (combinations of 8 to 10 techniques) to paragraphs of several sentences to short essays (kata). In these exercises the main study is of the spaces between the techniques, not so much to what happens during each technique.

a. COMBINATIONS. Combinations are sequences of techniques introduced to karate classes by the instructor, who usually makes them up just before class. At PSI, most class sessions end with a new combination to promote mobility and creativity with body language.

Exercise IC-15

Try the following combination. First, do each technique step by step, until the combination is barely learned. Second, do it slowly and continuously about five times. Third, do the combination rapidly to get a feeling of the total pattern:
[counter-punch (R,N)]-
[front-snap-kick (R)]-
[step-into counter-punch (L)],
[step-back side-stance (W) high-inside-forearm-block (R,N)]-
[step-to front-stance (W) counter-down-block (R,N)]-
[side-snap-kick (R,N)]-
[reverse-half-body counter-up-block (L,N)]-
[step-into counter-knife-hand-strike-lock (R,N) neck].
Fourth, teach yourself the mirror image. First go slowly, starting with the right-leg forward and right hand in down-block, making small adjustments for the left to right interchange. Then do the mirror image fast.

b. TWO-PERSON COMBINATIONS. For advanced students, I have created two-person combinations to bridge the gap between combinations, the study of the interplay between the body and imagination, and the strategic interplay encountered in sparring. Because they are quite difficult to do, mistakes often occur. However, when both partners react correctly, tremendous feedback pertaining to attention and physical techniques is available. The two opponents learn both sides independently, but learn the mirror image by doing it slowly together. The two opponents in the following Exercise are labelled B and C. Both sides should appreciate that their attention should be engaged in the interaction of B and C, implicitly labelled as A:

Exercise IC-16

[B: kneeling (S)]
&[C: kneeling (N)]

[B: on-knee (L,W) counter-high-inside-round-block (L,S)]
&[C: on-knee (R) counter-punch face (R,N)]

[B: from-floor (E) side-thrust-kick (L,E) groin]
&[C: step-in (N) round-kick (R)]

[C: front-stance (R,N) down-block (L,SW)]
&[B: on-knee (R) strike-lock (L,NE) ribs]

[C: [step-away (N)]-[turn-to two-hand-sweep-block (S) on-knee (L,S)]]
&[B: still-on-knee side-thrust-kick (L,NE) back-of-knee]

[C: round-kick (R) from floor (S)]
&[B: from-floor leaning-away (NW) up-block (R,N)]

[C: leg-back kneeling (S) strike-snap (L) face]
&[B: up-to-kneeling (N) counter-punch (L) stomach]

c. KATA. The study of kata can be usefully separated into two kinds of practices, the study of smooth body motions and the study of various attention states. The application of the physical laws of momentum and energy allow you to smoothly connect techniques, forming patterns of body movement.

Exercise IC-17

Do the [kata] emphasising the uses of continuity of momentum and energy of compression and energy.

Exercise IC-18

The kata can be used to understand the basic relationships one has with the external environment and to practice the correct use of the imagination. Although the form is "memorized," one does not consciously think of each technique just before it is executed. Rather, as the unconscious mind "reels off" the kata projected into real space, the conscious mind, acting through the body, spontaneously reacts to the up-coming image. Practice this technique by shifting or rocking from side to side -- being in motion helps to maximize the mind-body connection. Between two to four heart-beats, allow some imaginary stimulus from the left, right, or front to cause you to react with a block-attack sequence. Similarly, the kata is done correctly by synchronizing the information from the imagination (unconscious) with a barely conscious concentrated reaction.

Now practice the kata by starting with over-all awareness. Your unconscious "tells" you the technique. You spontaneously begin and continue to concentrate towards focus. You return to awareness-all-over and exercise imagination. Then you continue to concentrate to the next focus, and so on. Try to feel this attention cycle (awareness-imagination-concentration-awareness ...) flow smoothly through the kata.

Exercise IC-19

There are so many things to remember to do in practicing the kata: Individual techniques; overall rhythm; synchronization of energy and momentum; synchronization of body and mind. However, just do the kata, and afterwards, look back to find the "holes" -- i.e., which of the above things were done incorrectly (not up to par, for you, at this time). Then practice the kata by emphasizing the "hole" -- i.e., momentum, or awareness, etc. Now do the kata again by merging yourself with your environment.

Exercise IC-20

To use the learned kata to more closely stimulate "defense against surprise attack," do the kata in mirror image (right instead of left, and left instead of right). React to your imagination and do the techniques and rhythm as well as possible without allowing frustration, confusion, or other negative feelings to interfere with the natural flow. The use of mirror image illustrates that the kata has an abstract pattern of its own. Its physical manifestation in mirror image feels different to the muscles from the original form. However, the pattern is not really different.

If a combination has a main theme -- an overall body or mental feeling -- and a few minor themes, it may rightfully be called a kata. There are many kata that have been practiced for the last several hundred years. These kata are used for standardized testing -- to give students an honest evaluation of their current level of performance. The kata should not be treated as an abstract sequence of exercises merely to be memorized. Indeed, strategies of defense and attack, sustained attention, and body flexibility and coordination are but a few important reasons for practicing the same kata hundreds and thousands of times.

For the convenience of the novice reading this book, the first Shotokan kata, Heian #1, or "Heian Shodan," is given:

Exercise IC-21

[natural-stance (N) fists-closed],

[down-block (L,W)],

[step-in-punch (R,W)],

[step-back down-block (R,E)],

[bring blocking-hand and the front-leg back through center line of the body]-[strike-down (R) collar-bone]-

[step-in-punch (L,E)],

[down-block (L,N)],

[step-in up-block (R,N)],

[step-in up-block (L,N)]-

[step-in up-block (R,N) !],

[turn (L,E) down-block (L,E)],

[step-in punch (R,E)],

[step-back (W) down-block (R,W)],

[step-in punch (L,W)],

[down-block (L,S)],

[step-in punch (R,S)],

[step-in punch (L,S)]-

[step-in punch (R,S) !],

[turn (L,W) back-stance knife-hand-block (L,W)],

[step-in (R,NW) knife-hand-block (R,NW)],

[turn (R,E) knife-hand-block (R,E)],

[step-in (L,NE) knife-hand-block (L,NE)],

[step back (L) to start (N)].

Among all the many forms, 25 are very well known to Shotokan instructors. An occasional advanced work-out might include all these forms. They comprise almost 1000 movements, a reasonable measure of a good workout. These forms are:

Bassai Dai, Sho
Chintei
Empi
Gankaku
Gojushiho Dai, Sho
Hangetsu
Heian #1, #2, #3, #4, #5
Jion
Jitte
Kanku Dai, Sho
Meikyo
Niju shiho
Sochin
Tekki #1, #2, #3
Unsu
Wankan

Exercise IC-22

e. IMPROVISATION. After some techniques have been developed, one can find and refine the intuitive patterns that are usually barely lurking in the unconscious by practicing [improvisation]. This is done by continuously sparring for several minutes -- preset by a timer -- with imagined opponents responding to their rhythms spontaneously projected into the external environment. In this exercise, there is no room for several journeys between focal and global attention, or between external and internal patterns to shape strategies. One's intuitions developed during previous practice sessions become stark and apparent. It is these intuitions that most probably would be used at the present time to form strategies and responses in sparring or self-defense situations. New intuitions and desirable modifications, corrections, or transformations of old intuitions may now be developed and naturalized by creating, and creatively learning, new combinations stressing your weaknesses.

f. T'AI CHI. All advanced kata include some slow, smooth movements to stress attention and body dynamics. An important complementary training to karate can be found in T'ai Chi. Both the Wu and Yang styles are recommended, the latter stressing grounded techniques similar to karate, and the former stressing larger movements perhaps better suited to give feedback to the novice.

g. Bibliography. A few books are recommended for additional study:

S. Delza, *T'ai Chi Chu'an* (Cornerstone Library, New York, 1961) presents the Wu style long form.

G. Funakoshi, *Karate-Do Kyohan,* translated by T. Ohshima (Kodansha Int. Ltd., New York, 1973) presents many of the basic Shotokan kata.

L. Ingber, *The Karate Instructor's Handbook* (ISA, Solana Beach, CA, 1976) presents many combinations and two-person-combinations, enough for a year's practice. There are several "typos," so try them alone first before trying them in class. Copies of these combinations which appear in Appendix 4 (20 pages) may be obtained by sending $3.50 to cover costs incurred for copying, postage and handling to PSI, Drawer W, Solana Beach, CA 92075.

Y. Ming-Shi, *Tai-Chi Chuan for Health and Beauty* (Bunka, Tokyo, 1976) presents the Yang style short form.

M. Musashi, *A Book of Five Rings,* translated by V. Harris (Overlook Press, Woodstock, New York, 1974) presents the body and attention strategies of Mushashi.

N. Nakayama, *Best Karate* (Kodansha Int. Ltd., New York, 1979) presents an ongoing series of Shotokan kata, beginning with book #5.

PART II. TRAINING DYNAMICS

This part of the book gives training schedules which, when appropriately modified to accommodate individual students and instructors, should be useful for many years of training.

Chapter IIA contains a four week beginner cycle, to be repeated three times during the first twelve weeks of a thirteen week (one quarter of a year) intermediate cycle given in Chapter IIB. Chapter IIC gives advanced class exercises for students who are assumed to be continuing their training in an additional class similar to the intermediate class.

ROTATING STUDENTS. From my observations on different schools, a short note on rotating opponents is essential to aid instructors who wish to maximize sparring interactions among their students: All those students who are to spar with each other should be first grouped together. Sometimes this may include all the students present, sometimes only a particular belt level, etc. In each group observe the following rules: If the number of students is an even number, that is, a number divisible by 2, have them face each other in two equal rows. Students will move clockwise around these rows, as if they were all holding on to a large rope circling around their backs. Imagine a big red "X" painted on the ground under each student. Pick one member, at either end of either row, to be "fixed." That person will always come back to his or her "X" when the group is ready to rotate to new spots and new opponents. At that time, all other students move one "X" space over in a clockwise direction. One person will have to skip over the space taken by the "fixed" person because that space is considered to be already occupied.

If the number of students in a group is odd, then again line up the students in two facing rows, but now with an empty space at either end of either row. When you draw your imaginary red "X"s, also draw one on this empty space. This empty space is now your "fixed" space. When changing opponents, everyone rotates as before, respecting the occupation of this "fixed" space. The person facing the "fixed" space can move to a corner of the room and stand in [side-stance], or follow along using the closest facing person as a distant opponent.

If you follow these simple rules, then every full cycle of rotation will always enable each student to spar or exercise with every other student, once and only once per cycle.

IIA. Beginner Dynamics

This chapter presents a four-week course of study for beginners, to introduce them to the basic body and attention dynamics required at the next level of study. My personal philosophy has always been to treat each beginner as a potential black belt. I believe that few rewards are as meaningful to a student as accomplishing skills that he or she objectively knows are difficult to perform. Also, no matter how long it takes, each student must eventually learn to do all techniques with power and precision. This is necessary to prevent accidents due to sloppy techniques. It is not as easy to erase mistakes performed with another person as it is when working with pencil and paper.

This beginner's course covers the most basic skills. Therefore, it is not surprising that many, if not most, intermediate and advanced students regularly drop in on this course to brush up on these skills. Although this adds lots of vital spirit to the class, care should be taken to keep these classes geared to the beginners.

Section IIA-0 is a one-time introductory class for a new student, whether a novice or an experienced practitioner from another school. Sections IIA-1-4 comprise a four-week cycle of beginner classes. Each class is typically given two or three times per week. Most students must repeat this four week cycle two or three times before being ready to start the intermediate classes given in Chapter IIB.

IIA-0. Introductory Class

The introductory class is the student's first formal introduction to a karate class. Usually an advanced Brown Belt or Black Belt is capable of giving this class, after going through several mock classes with the chief instructor. There are several things to be accomplished at this class:

a. PAPERWORK. Basic paperwork essential for administration should be initiated: Class hours, explanation of rates and fees, and levels of instruction offered are essential data to be given to the student. It is useful to gather some statistical information for the school's records: the student's age, profession or grade if a student, previous martial arts' experience, where the student learned of your school, his or her reasons for joining, goals to achieve a specific level of proficiency or colored belt, etc. The need for rigid discipline should be explained, highlighting its necessity for safety and respect for classmates, and its importance to promote complete attention to the class activity.

b. MEDITATION. Students should be told how to [meditate] and [bow] with the class, and by themselves if they come in late or if they must leave class early. The formal ceremony basically consists of three parts: [Concentrate] is some command, given by the highest belted student, directing each student to concentrate to a point in front and 45 degrees down from his or her head. This is to gather attention and spirit for the coming class, or to gather oneself at the end of class. [Attention] is some command, given by the same person a short while later, to direct attention to include the external surroundings which the student must presently deal with. [Bow] is some command to bow, to show respect to fellow classmates and to the instructor(s).

c. WARM-UP. The [warm-up] is designed to loosen up the student's joints and to stretch the muscles. It should not be done in a jerky fashion or at a fast pace. The student should experience at least a small moment of relaxation at the height of each stretch. The following [warm-up] is designed to start at the top of the spine, and work downwards:

Exercise IIA-1

[Natural-stance].
[Jumping-jacks].
[Neck: move forward and back, turn side to side, roll in circles].
[Swing arms forward and back, stretching chest and back].
[Whip arms around in circles, first one direction, then the other].
[Twist side to side, keeping legs straight, not locking knees].
[Side-bends, stretching to a long distance away, to each side].
[Forward-bends].
[Back-bends].
[Roll the torso in circles about the hips, alternating directions].
[Stretch under each leg, keeping one leg flat on the floor while squatting on it, and gently pulling on the other straightened leg which is resting with its heel touching the floor].
[Stretch inside each leg by pushing sidewards while in a long [front-stance], but with feet parallel as in [side-stance]].
[Give pressure to the ankles by touching the feet together and pushing on the knees, gently rocking forward, and then rolling the bent knees in circles].
[Gently repeatedly bend and straighten the knees, aided by pressure from the hands].
[Sitting on the floor in a "jack-knife" or "V" position with the torso and feet straight off the floor, [punch] 10 or 20 times].
[Stand up and shake out ankles and wrists].

d. OVERVIEW TUTORIAL. The main purpose of the introductory class is to generally acquaint the new student with the nature of the skills required, and not so much to rigorously teach these skills. This tutorial works as well with several students as it does with one. The next sub-section after this one is for a student with previous experience.

Exercise IIA-2

Demonstrate for the student the power possible with correct technique. Explain the four power methods in:
[Side-stance punch].
[Front-stance counter-punch].
[Front-stance counter-punch], [down-block]-[counter-punch].
[Step-in punch], [step-back back-stance knife-hand-block]-[step-in punch].

Exercise IIA-3

Explain making a [fist], tensing the body from the floor upwards, and pulling the fingers closed. Practice this while breathing out. Do this faster and faster, then with kiai [! fist]. Explain and correct tucking under the hips.

Exercise IIA-4

Take [side-stance]. Make [fist] with hands to the sides held head-height. [* Punch] slowly, emphasising breathing and coordination: Start both hands in motion together with the beginning of body compression, and end all movement at the same time. Now fast, [punch]. [Up-block] a few times. Then try [outside-round-block]. Then [down-block]. Stand up and shake out the ankles.

Exercise IIA-5

Adjust [front-stance]. From [natural-stance], drive forward to [front-stance] several times. Push into the student's outstretched arms while he or she is in [front-stance]. Stress the importance of stance, posture and hip-connection.

In [front-stance], try [up-block],[counter-punch]. Then try [down-block],[counter-punch].

Exercise IIA-6

From [side-stance], move into [back-stance]. Then try [back-stance (N)],[back-stance (S)]. Add [down-block] to this movement, then [knife-hand-block].

Exercise IIA-7

Try shifting from [counter-punch],[step-in counter-punch]. Then try [step-in punch],[step-in punch]. Briefly point out the importance of the pulling hand. Explain the necessity of quick reactions and count sharply.

The next two exercises are optional, and their inclusion depends on whether there is time left to practice them.

Exercise IIA-8

Start by a wall, preferably marked with a point. Practice distance control by doing [natural-stance], [step-back back-stance knife-hand-block], [front-stance counter-punch].

Exercise IIA-9

Try the inside-tension stance [half-moon-stance]. Try [half-moon-stance outside-round-block], [half-moon-stance counter-punch].

Exercise IIA-10

[Meditate]. [Bow]. Answer any questions. You should also have a standard offer to loan some karate text in return for a refundable deposit.

I require students to take the introductory class even if they plan to attend only a weekly self-defense class, as outlined in Section IIB-14. Once they see just how much training is required to perform even simple techniques, novices can better appreciate the reason and necessity of attempting only the simplest techniques as practiced in the self-defense class.

e. ADVANCED TUTORIAL. Occasionally, an experienced student from another area or school will wish to join your class. It is still reasonable for you to require an introductory tutorial, to familiarize this student with your class and the way you expect techniques to be performed, etc. However, this tutorial is also a chance for you to observe whether this student can really advance to your intermediate class or to your advanced class. If in doubt, you owe it to this student and to your class to require more beginner class training.

Exercise IIA-11

Proceed as before with the general paperwork, discussion, etc. [Meditate]. [Bow]. [Warm-up]. Then go through the following exercises at a standard class pace:

Exercise IIA-12

In [side-stance], do each of the following several times: [Punch]. [Up-block]. [Down-block]. [Knife-hand-block]. [Inside-round-block]. [Outside-round-block].

Exercise IIA-13

In [front-stance], do [knife-hand-strike-lock face],[counter-strike-snap stomach].

Exercise IIA-14

Face each other and do Exercise IC-4: [A: counter-punch]&[D: counter-punch].

Exercise IIA-15

Practice rhythm control, [stepping-in] three times: [punch],[punch]-[punch].
Then try [punch]-[punch],[punch].

Exercise IIA-16

[[Step-back up-block]/[step-back outside-round-block]]-[counter-punch].
[Step-back outside-round-block],[step-in back-stance knife-hand-block]-[counter-punch].

Exercise IIA-17

[Three-step-sparring]: Attack side has choice of three targets each step,
[face]/[stomach]/[groin], and also a choice of two rhythms, [[...],[...]-[...]]/[[...]-[...],[...]]. Defense side must do [D: [block]-/,[block],/-[block]-[counter-punch stomach]].

Exercise IIA-18

Review the basic kicks, several times on each side (R,L):
[Front-thrust-kick]-[leg back],[front-knee-kick]-[leg back],[front-snap-kick]-[leg back]-[counter-punch].
[Side-thrust-kick]-[leg back],[side-knee-kick]-[leg back],[side-snap-kick]-[leg back]-[counter-snap-strike].
[Crescent-kick]-[leg back],[round-knee-kick]-[leg back],[round-snap-kick]-[leg back]-[counter-knife-hand-strike-lock face].

Exercise IIA-19

[A: [kick]-[punch]/[strike]]&[D: [lateral-shift block]-[counter-punch]].

Exercise IIA-20

Practice timing and distance control with kicks:
[A: [step-in punch],(#1)[in-place punch face]]&[D: (#1)[front-thrust-kick]].
[A: [step-in punch],(#1)[step-back punch face]]&[D: [step-back block],(#1)[front-thrust-kick]].
[A: [counter-punch],(#1)[step-in counter-punch face]]&[D: (#1)[front-thrust-kick]].

Exercise IIA-21

Examine the student's most current [kata].

Exercise IIA-22

Create a 7 to 9 step combination, as described in Section IC-3a, and have the student learn and perform it.

Exercise IIA-23

[Meditate]. [Bow]. Answer any questions.

IIA-1. Front-Stance, Counter-Punch, Timing

The main two points of this week's classes are to give the new student appreciation and respect for the integrity of a correct body technique and the interaction context invariably required of such techniques. Although there are many new techniques and several important principles of body kinematics to learn in this short four week cycle, I consider these two points so important, that I believe it worthwhile to explore the depth of just one technique, [front-stance counter-punch stomach].

This class alternates successively deeper studies of [counter-punch] with the timing Exercise IC-3: [A: counter-punch]&[D: counter-punch]. This timing exercise gives motivation to perform a correct body technique, and it also makes the student aware that the context of any body technique always requires a sensitive sharing of attention, between one's own technique/strategy and that of one's opponent.

Exercise IIA-24

[Meditate]. [Bow]. [Warm-up].

Exercise IIA-25

Do Exercise IC-3, correcting distance and posture. Explain how to "see" an opponent: Try to simultaneously look at his or her eyes and shoulders. This will put him or her slightly out of focus. In return for losing a bit of detail using your central vision, you will gain a complete image of your opponent and become more visually sensitive to his or her movements using your peripheral vision.

Exercise IIA-26

Concentrate on [before-stance] of [front-stance counter-punch stomach]. Attempt to develop maximum initial speed of [hip-rotation] to add to the [punch].

Exercise IIA-27

Concentrate on [after-stance] to develop a strong mass connection into the ground. At the focus of [punch], gently push back on the extended arm, giving direct feedback on poor posture, stiff shoulders, loose hips, and sloppy stance. Beginning with the next class, given in the next section, this feedback should be given in the opposite order, starting with the base, and proceeding to the target.

Exercise IIA-28

Develop an appreciation for the smooth, continuous transition between [before-stance], developing speed, and [after-stance], developing mass. The following analogy has proven to be useful: Consider the torso as a tube of toothpaste. The analogy to strongly squeezing out the toothpaste is to strongly squeeze the arm out of the torso and stance. During the middle of the technique, the body works continually to accelerate the arm, gaining more and more speed. Near the end, however, just as the toothpaste tube becomes empty and rigid, so the body becomes a rigid mass from the inside of the abdomen to to the target.

Again do Exercise IIA-25, stressing getting to the target quickly, but with a more respectable technique than before.

Exercise IIA-29

Have the class face each other in two rows. A student in one row will give explicit feedback to the student facing him or her regarding the strength and continuity of the transition between [before-stance] and [after-stance] during [front-stance counter-punch stomach]. If both people are facing each other [front-stance (L)], this is accomplished by the student who is giving feedback by pushing with the left hand on the opponent's [punching (R)] hand, and by pulling with the right hand with an equal force on the opponent's pulling (L) hand. Only a little force on each hand is required, enough to make the opponent's punching and pulling hands take about two seconds to complete their course. The attacking opponent can better appreciate corrections to poor posture, stiff shoulders, loose hips, and sloppy stance, and thereby appreciate how the [stance] and [hip-rotation] are essential to make power. After doing each impeded [counter-punch] three or four times, have the opponents separate a few feet apart, and then let the attacker try to [counter-punch] as if he or she were still being impeded. The idea is to apply the same force used in resisting the former impedance, but now used to continually accelerate the body and limbs.

Exercise IIA-30

Again do Exercise IIA-25. Have the attack side attempt to test his or her perception of the opponent: During two to four heartbeats, the attacker makes a conscious decision whether to [counter-punch] when the opponent is either ready or not ready to [D: counter-punch]. Only by testing this perception many times with many opponents can one be sure one's perceptions are correct. It is many times as important to cause your opponent to move, as it is to sense a "dead" spot for you to dive into with an attack. The concepts of [feints] and [counter-attacking] are currently appreciated by all professional competitive athletes.

At the second or third class, if time permits, some practice may be done with [up-block] and [down-block].

Exercise IIA-31

[Meditate]. [Bow].

IIA-2. Punching, Blocking, Heian #1, Three-Step-Sparring

The main two points of this second week's practice are to give the student enough techniques to perform the kata Heian #1 and to to engage in simple sparring.

Exercise IIA-32

[Meditate]. [Bow]. [Warm-up].

Exercise IIA-33

Practice the following hand techniques in [side-stance]: [Punch]. [Up-block]. [Down-block]. [Knife-hand-block]. [Inside-round-block]. [Outside-round-block].

Exercise IIA-34

Practice both methods of [hip-rotation]:
[Natural-stance   (N)]-[step-to-side]-[front-stance   (W/E)   direct-rotation   down-block],[counter-punch (W/E)].
[Natural-stance   (N)]-[step-back]-[front-stance   (N)   reverse-rotation   down-block],[counter-punch (N)].

Exercise IIA-35

Practice [hip-shifting]:
[Front-stance counter-punch],[step-in counter-punch].
[Step-in punch],[step-in punch]-[step-in punch].

Exercise IIA-36

Practice [three-step-sparring]:
[A: [step-in punch (R) face],[step-in punch stomach]-[step-in punch groin]]
&[D: [step-back up-block (L)],[step-back outside-round-block]-[step-back down-block]-[counter-punch stomach]].

Exercise IIA-37

Practice [back-stance]: [Side-stance (N)],[back-stance (W) knife-hand-block (L)],[back-stance (E) knife-hand-block (R)],....
[Step-in front-stance punch],[step-back back-stance knife-hand-block].

Exercise IIA-38

Teach [Heian #1]; see Exercise IC-21.

Exercise IIA-39

[Meditate]. [Bow].

IIA-3. Thrust-Kicks

The main point of this third week is to teach hip-thrusting techniques using the legs.

Exercise IIA-40

[Meditate]. [Bow]. [Warm-up].

Exercise IIA-41

Review Exercise IIA-33.

Exercise IIA-42

Review and correct [Heian #1].

Exercise IIA-43

Do [front-thrust-kick] in three stages:

First, do the kicking trajectory slowly, learning the relative timing and movements of the legs and hips:
[Front-stance]-[* pick-up kicking-leg],[* extend-hips thrust-kick],[* pull-back-leg-to-hips],[* push-leg-back]-[front-stance].

Second, learn to use the abdomen to bring the leg to hip-center, and to use the stance (other) leg to project the kicking leg away from hip-center:
[Front-stance]-[use-abdomen pick-up-leg],[use-stance thrust-hip-and-leg],[use-abdomen pull-back-leg to center],[use-stance push-leg-back]-[front-stance].

Third, learn to use the abdomen and stance simultaneously to get a smooth strong kick:
[Front-stance]-[pick-up-leg]&[thrust-hip-and-leg],[pull-back-leg to center]&[push-leg-back]-[front-stance].

Exercise IIA-44

Follow the order of Exercise IIA-43 for [side-thrust-kick]:
[Front-stance (N)]-[* pick-up-leg (N)],[* extend-hips kick (E/W)],[* pull-back leg],[* push-leg-back]-[front-stance].
[Pick-up leg],[thrust-kick],[pull-back leg],[push-back]-[front-stance].
[Pick-up leg]&[side-thrust-kick],[pull-back leg]&[push-back]-[front-stance].

Exercise IIA-45

Follow the order of Exercise IIA-43 for [back-thrust-kick].

Exercise IIA-46

Do [two-step-sparring] with these kicks. Attack side start in [counter-punch (S)] position, defense side in [natural-stance (N)]:
[A: [front-thrust-kick stomach]-[counter-punch face (SE)]
&[D: [step-to-side down-block (NW)]-[counter-punch stomach]].

[A: [reverse-rotation side-thrust-kick stomach]-[turn-hips]-[counter-punch face (SW)]]
&[D: [step-to-outside-of-kick down-block (NE)]-[counter-punch ribs]].

[A: [front-thrust-kick/side-thrust-kick counter-punch (SE/SW)]
&[D: [step-to-correct-side down-block (NW/NE)]-counter-punch]].

Exercise IIA-47

[Meditate]. [Bow].
For the first class of the week, do Exercises IIA-43-44-45 holding onto a bar/wall for balance. For the second/third class, do these exercises with arms folded, holding both elbows. Tension and motion in the arms or shoulders indicates disrupting use of faulty reaction forces in the head and shoulders. The upper torso should remain relaxed throughout the kicks.

IIA-4. Striking Techniques, Lateral-Shifting

The main point of the fourth week is to teach rotation and whipping techniques using the arms, legs and body.

Exercise IIA-48

[Meditate]. [Bow]. [Warm-up].

Exercise IIA-49

Review Exercise IIA-33.

Exercise IIA-50

Review and correct [Heian #1].

Exercise IIA-51

Compare [down-block] with [bottom-fist-strike-lock]:
[Natural-stance (N)]-[front-stance (W/E) down-block]. Explain the importance of driving the elbow through the center of the body to get maximum speed at focus.
[Natural-stance (N)]-[front-stance (W/E) bottom-fist-strike-lock face].

Exercise IIA-52

Develop [strike-snap]:
[Natural-stance (N)]-[front-stance (W/E) elbow-strike (W/E)]. Keep fist bent close to line of upper-arm, and keep elbow driving to target along a line including the hip-center. While in this position, apply [hip-vibration], vibrating the stance, hips and upper-arm, but keeping the forearm free to snap to and snap-back from the target.
[Natural-stance (N)]-[front-stance (W/E) bottom-fist-strike-snap (W/E) face].

Exercise IIA-53

Similarly, teach [front-snap-kick]: [Front-stance]-[front-thrust-kick], [leg-back front-stance], [front-knee-kick], [leg-back front-stance], [front-snap-kick], [leg-back front-stance]. The first day, do this holding onto a bar/wall for balance. The second/third day, follow up the last technique with -[counter-punch].

Exercise IIA-54

Similarly, teach [round-snap-kick]: [Front-stance]-[crescent-kick opposite-palm], [leg-back front-stance], [round-knee-kick], [leg-back front-stance], [round-snap-kick], [leg-back front-stance]. The second/third day, follow up the last technique with -[counter-knife-hand-strike-lock].

Exercise IIA-55

Similarly teach [side-snap-kick]: [Front-stance (N)]-[side-thrust-kick (W/E)], [leg-back front-stance (N)], [side-knee-kick (W/E)], [leg-back front-stance (N)], [side-snap-kick (W/E)], [leg-back front-stance (N)]. The second/third day, follow up the last technique with -[bottom-fist-strike-snap (W/E)].

Exercise IIA-56

Practice [circle-shifting outside-round-block], swinging the back leg through center, around towards your back, to a new [front-stance] at an angle of 90 degrees from the last position. Then [counter-punch]. Make two or three full circles with each leg, in quarter-circle increments.

Exercise IIA-57

Practice [side-shifting down-block], stepping through center to a new [front-stance] at an angle 90 degrees from the last position. Then [counter-punch]. Make two or three full circles with each leg, in quarter-circle increments.

Exercise IIA-58

Do exercise IIA-46, but with [front-snap-kick] instead of [front-thrust-kick], and with [direct-rotation side-snap-kick] instead of [reverse-rotation side-thrust-kick].

Exercise IIA-59

[Meditate]. [Bow].

IIB. Intermediate Dynamics

This chapter presents a thirteen week course of study for intermediate students, to teach the body and attention dynamics described in the Introduction and in Chapter IC. There is also enough basic practice of techniques such that the elements of Chapters IA-B are also continually trained.

The general approach of each training session is to first practice some exercises that give specific feedback on the theme of the week. Then, typically, there are sparring exercises that require spontaneous decision-making among strategies exercising this theme. The exercises are rigorous enough so that feedback is also given on proper body kinematics.

Each class begins with: [Meditate]. [Bow]. [Warm-up] (described in Exercise IIA-1). Each class ends with [Meditate]. [Bow]. Most of these classes are designed to leave about ten to fifteen minutes at the end of an hour session, for the practice of a new combination created by the instructor, as described in Exercise IC-15. The combination should also reflect the theme of the week. Over the course of the thirteen week cycle, the instructor should also arrange that all the basic techniques described in Chapter IB have been properly practiced, by supplementing the other class exercises with these combinations.

After the initial [warm-up], from week 2 on, students do their own [kata] several times, as they learned it during week 1. This is an additional warm-up, as well as a necessary rehearsal of learned techniques. Sparring exercises can immediately follow with an added margin of safety after this physical and mental preparation.

Each numbered section in this chapter defines a week's practice. Section IIB-14 is an optional self-defense class to be given the thirteenth week, or to be given as a separate ongoing class for all members, novices through experts. Similarly, Section IIB-15 presents an optional class in t'ai chi stick-sparring to promote rhythm practice.

For most weeks, there will be sub-sections a, b and c corresponding to three sessions per week. Generally, Sub-Section b includes some of Sub-Section a for review, Sub-Section c merges Sub-Sections a and b for review, and each sub-section typically offers a different variation of the week's theme.

IIB-1. Kata and Basic Sparring

This is the first week of a yearly quarter of thirteen weeks, and continuity is necessary to connect to the previous quarter. Many students have probably passed their exams, described in Section IIB-13, and they must now learn their new kata for this quarter. Advanced students can help to teach the several groups that require this training.

a,b,c. First Exercise

[Meditate]. [Bow]. [Warm-up].

Exercise IIB-1

All sessions this week include a rigorous training in [kata]. Students who didn't pass their exams obviously need repeated instruction on their [kata]. Depending on how fast students learn their kata, you can progress from stressing the outline of the form, to its rhythm, to some more subtle points in body and attentional techniques.

Exercise IIB-2

This is also an opportunity to correct some deficiencies observed in the class as a whole during the previous exam. This usually reflects on something systematically missing in the course of instruction. Basic sparring, at the level required in the exam, is a good exercise to give students feedback on simple, and therefore important body techniques, because the most deeply learned techniques are those that typically surface.

If the lowest level belt in any engagement is a White Belt, both sides practice [three-step-sparring]. If the lowest level is a Green Belt, both sides practice [one-step-sparring], with the defense starting in [natural-stance]. If the lowest level is a Brown Belt or Black Belt, practice [semi-free-one-step-sparring], with both sides starting in [free-stance], and the attack side attempting to [feint] before driving in with his or her single attacks.

Final Exercise

[Combination]. [Meditate]. [Bow].

IIB-2. Punching Combinations

Punching combinations are practiced, emphasising focusing at different distances, and to targets that may have to be approached from angular trajectories. After this drill, students attempt to apply these techniques as sparring strategies.

a. First Exercise

[Meditate]. [Bow]. [Warm-up]. [Kata].

Exercise IIB-3

Practice [punch] at different distances. Emphasis is on adjusting body timing to achieve focus at different distances:
[Up-block]-[counter-punch stomach].
[Outside-round-block]-[vertical-punch].
[Down-block]-[close-punch].

Exercise IIB-4

Practice other punching trajectories:
[Round-punch face]-[counter-rising-punch].
[Front-stance counter-round-punch (N)]-[side-stance (N) hook-punch (L/R,E/W)].

Exercise IIB-5

Spar at a pace smooth enough to permit students to try different [punches] at different distances and angles:
[A: [step-in punch]-[punch]]
&[D: [block]-[punch]].
Alternate A and D after each engagement, continuously.

Final Exercise

[Combination]. [Meditate]. [Bow].

b. First Exercise

[Meditate]. [Bow]. [Warm-up]. [Kata].

Exercise IIB-6

Do exercises similar to Exercises IIB-3-4.

Exercise IIB-7

[A: [punch]-[punch],[block]-[punch]]
&[D: [block]-[block],[punch]-[punch]].
Alternate A and D after each engagement, continuously.

Final Exercise

[Combination]. [Meditate]. [Bow].

c. First Exercise

[Meditate]. [Bow]. [Warm-up]. [Kata].

Exercise IIB-8

Do exercises similar to Exercises IIB-3-4.

Exercise IIB-9

[A: [punch straight-trajectory]-[punch straight-trajectory]]
&[D: [lateral-shift block]-[punch curved-trajectory]].

Final Exercise

[Combination]. [Meditate]. [Bow].

IIB-3. Move-Pause Sparring Rhythms

The point of this week's training is to have students appreciate how [no-movement] is as important as [movement], and how these two techniques can be strung together to produce viable strategic sparring rhythms.

a. First Exercise

[Meditate]. [Bow]. [Warm-up]. [Kata].

Exercise IIB-10

[Step-in punch], [step-in punch]-[step-in punch].
[Up-block], [counter-punch]-[step-in counter-strike-snap].

Exercise IIB-11

First, follow an opponent's rhythm, keeping just out of attack-range, then counter-attack keeping the same time lapse between his or her last attack and your counter-attack, as existed between his or her first two attacks. All punches can be in place or stepping in:
[A: [punch]-/, [punch]]
&[D: [move]-/, [move]-/, [punch]]].

Exercise IIB-12

Second, cut into your opponent's rhythm, attacking between his or her first two or last two attacks:
[A: [punch]-/,(#1)[punch]-/,(#2)[punch]]
&[D: [[move]-[(#1) punch]]/[[move]-/,[move]-[(#2) punch]]].

Final Exercise

[Combination]. [Meditate]. [Bow].

b. First Exercise

[Meditate]. [Bow]. [Warm-up]. [Kata].

Exercise IIB-13

Do exercises similar to Exercises IIB-10-11-12.

Exercise IIB-14

Use [D: [counter-kick]] instead of [D: [punch]] in Exercises IIB-11-12.

Final Exercise

[Combination]. [Meditate]. [Bow].

c. First Exercise

[Meditate]. [Bow]. [Warm-up]. [Kata].

Exercise IIB-15

Do exercises similar to Exercises IIB-11-12-14.

Exercise IIB-16

Do variations of [three-step-sparring]:
[A: [step-in punch]-/,[step-in punch],/-[step-in punch]]
&[D: [block]-/,[block],/-[block]-[counter-punch]].

Exercise IIB-17

As a variation of Exercise IIB-16, after each [block], D [counter-attacks]. Person A moves in for each [step-in-punch] after the focus of D's [counter-attack], but to a preplanned rhythm of [A: [1]-/,[2],/-[3]]. That is, after the first [D: counter-attack], A may wait until the body of D has relaxed its compression, and then [A: step-in punch]; after the second [D: counter-attack], A then uses the opposite trigger to [punch], right on D's compression. Or, A may [punch] off the compression of the first [D: counter-attack], and then [punch] on the space just after the compression of the second [D: counter-attack].

Final Exercise

[Combination]. [Meditate]. [Bow].

IIB-4. One-Step-Sparring

The main point is to build an appreciation for single, strong, precise techniques necessary to complement a sparring strategy. For reasons discussed in the Introduction, just before each interaction, both sides should show as little motion to the opponent as possible, but keep the feeling inside as if he or she were already in motion from a previous technique.

a. First Exercise

[Meditate]. [Bow]. [Warm-up]. [Kata].

Exercise IIB-18

First, D starts in [natural-stance] and studies timing to move against A's attack:
[A: punch]&[D: [block]-[counter-attack]].
[A: thrust-kick]&[D: [block]-[counter-attack]].

Exercise IIB-19

Second, D starts in [free-stance] and learns to control distance and angle as well as timing. Repeat Exercise IIB-18.

Exercise IIB-20

Third, A [feints], making a sudden but uncompleted [shift] or [punch], just before his or her main [attack]. Repeat Exercise IIB-19.

Final Exercise

[Combination]. [Meditate]. [Bow].

b. First Exercise

[Meditate]. [Bow]. [Warm-up]. [Kata].

Exercise IIB-21

Repeat Exercises IIB-18-19.

Exercise IIB-22

Do exercise similar to Exercise IIB-20, but with [A: punch] replaced by [A: [punch]/[strike]] and with [A: thrust-kick] replaced by [A: kick].

Final Exercise

[Combination]. [Meditate]. [Bow].

c. First Exercise

[Meditate]. [Bow]. [Warm-up]. [Kata].

Exercise IIB-23

Do Exercises IIB-18-19-22.

Exercise IIB-24

Extend the feeling of [one-step-sparring] to [two-step-sparring]: [A: [attack]-[attack]]&[D: [block]-[block]-[counter-attack]].

Final Exercise

[Combination]. [Meditate]. [Bow].

IIB-5. Stance Combinations

Several short but intense combinations are practiced to exploit the strong points of different stances in the context of creating sparring rhythms.

a. First Exercise

[Meditate]. [Bow]. [Warm-up]. [Kata].

Exercise IIB-25

Distance and angle control is the theme:
[Counter-punch]-[slide-back back-stance knife-hand-block]-[slide-in counter-punch].
[Counter-punch (N)]-[side-shift (NE/NW) angular-side-stance inside-round-block]-[slide-in (NE/NW) counter-punch].
[Counter-punch (N)]-[circle-shift (NW/NE) half-moon-stance outside-round-block]-[slide-in (NE/NW) counter-punch].

Exercise IIB-26

Spar using the different stances practiced in the various contexts:
[A: [punch]-[block]-[punch]]&[D: [block]-[punch]-[punch]].

Final Exercise

[Combination]. [Meditate]. [Bow].

b. First Exercise

[Meditate]. [Bow]. [Warm-up]. [Kata].

Exercise IIB-27

Changing from inside- to outside-tension stances is the theme. Start as usual in [front-stance (N)]:
[Slide-in hour-glass-stance up-block]-[drive-forward front-stance counter-punch].
[Slide-back cat-stance knife-hand-down-block]-[drive-forward back-stance counter-punch]-[drive-forward front-stance strike-snap].
[Circle-shift (NE/NW) half-moon-stance outside-round-block]-[side-shift (NW/NE) angular-side-stance inside-round-block]-[slide-in (N) front-stance counter-punch].

Exercise IIB-28

Apply Exercise IIB-27 in sparring:
[A: [punch]-[kick]]&[D: [block]-[punch]].
[A: [kick]-[punch]]&[D: [block]-[kick]].

Final Exercise

[Combination]. [Meditate]. [Bow].

c. First Exercise

[Meditate]. [Bow]. [Warm-up]. [Kata].

Exercise IIB-29

Include [kicking] in Exercise IIB-25. Replace the first [counter-punch] in those three combinations with a [kick]:
[Front-snap-kick]-[...]-[...].
[Side-thrust-kick (E/W)]-[...]-[...].
[Round-snap-kick (N)]-[...]-[...].

Exercise IIB-30

Insert a kick before each combination in Exercise IIB-27:
[Front-thrust-kick]-[...]-[...].
[Side-snap-kick]-[...]-[...]-[...].
[Crescent-kick opposite-palm (N)]-[...]-[...]-[...].

Exercise IIB-31

Apply Exercises IIB-29-30 in the sparring Exercises IIB-26-28, but with A and D interchanged after each interaction, continuously.

Final Exercise

[Combination]. [Meditate]. [Bow].

IIB-6. Kicking Combinations

Both A and D must learn how to interact with [kicks] before they can strategically work with strong and fast kicking techniques in [sparring].

a. First Exercise

[Meditate]. [Bow]. [Warm-up]. [Kata].

Exercise IIB-32

Practice the basic [kicks]:
[Front-stance]-[front-thrust-kick]-[leg-back   front-stance]-[front-knee-kick]-[leg-back front-stance]-[front-snap-kick]-[leg-back front-stance]-[counter-punch].

[Front-stance (N)]-[side-thrust-kick (E/W)]-[leg-back front-stance]-[side-knee-kick (E/W)]-[leg-back front-stance]-[side-snap-kick (E/W)]-[leg-back front-stance]-[strike-snap (E/W)].

[Front-stance]-[crescent-kick opposite-palm]-[leg-back front-stance]-[round-knee-kick]-[leg-back front-stance]-[round-snap-kick]-[leg-back front-stance]-[counter-knife-hand-strike-lock].

Exercise IIB-33

Practice [lateral-shifting]&[sweep-block] against [kicks]. Defense starts in [natural-stance]:
[A: [front-thrust-kick]-[punch face]]
&[D: [side-shift sweep-down-block]-[counter-punch stomach]].

[A: [side-thrust-kick]-[strike face]]
&[D: [circle-shift sweep-outside-down-block outside-of-kick]-[counter-punch stomach]].

[A: [round-snap-kick (N)]-[leg-back (SE/SW)]-[counter-punch (NW/NE)]]
&[D: [step-in (SW/SE) counter-sweep-down-block inside-of-kick]-[drive-in (SE/SW) counter-punch stomach]].

Exercise IIB-34

[A: [[thrust-kick]-[snap-kick]-[punch face]]/[[snap-kick]-[thrust-kick]-[punch face]]]
&[D: [sweep-block]-[sweep-block]-[kick]].

Final Exercise

[Combination]. [Meditate]. [Bow].

b. First Exercise

[Meditate]. [Bow]. [Warm-up]. [Kata].

Exercise IIB-35

Do Exercise IIB-32.

Exercise IIB-36

Do Exercise IIB-33, with A's choice of [kick], and D trying to react with the correct strategy.

Exercise IIB-37

Practice [kick] timing:
[A: [counter-punch]-(#1)[short-punch face]]
&[D: [(#1) front-thrust-kick].

[A: [step-in punch]-(#1)[step-back short-punch face]
&[D: [step-back block]-[(#1) front-thrust-kick]].

[A: [counter-punch]-(#1)[step-in punch face]
&[D: [(#1) front-thrust-kick]].

Exercise IIB-38

[A: [punch]-[kick]]&[D: [block]-[punch]].
[A: [kick]-[punch]]&[D: [block]-[kick]].
After each interaction A and D interchange, continuously.

Final Exercise

[Combination]. [Meditate]. [Bow].

c. First Exercise

[Meditate]. [Bow]. [Warm-up]. [Kata].

Exercise IIB-39

Do Exercises IIB-32-38.

Exercise IIB-40

[A: [kick]-[punch]/[strike]-[kick]]
&[D: [block]-[block]-[punch]].
After each interaction A and D interchange, continuously.

Final Exercise

[Combination]. [Meditate]. [Bow].

IIB-7. Block-Kick-Punch Permutations

This week's exercises are designed to teach students to create strong rhythmic combinations by having new techniques emerge across the hip-center from the previous technique. For example, [punch]-[punch] is best performed by alternating hands, as the body quickly stiffens if one limb is repeatedly used. Similarly, other strategic considerations being equal, [kicks] are appropriate techniques to use before or after a hand techniques. Speed and time to reach a target is determined by power, not necessarily how close the attack begins.

a. First Exercise

[Meditate]. [Bow]. [Warm-up]. [Kata].

Exercise IIB-41

Practice permutations, different orderings, of [block]-[kick]-[punch], but ending with an [attack].
[Step-back up-block]-[front-snap-kick]-[punch].
[Step-back outside-round-block]-[step-in punch]-[side-thrust-kick].
[Step-in punch]-[step-back down-block]-[front-snap-kick].
[Front-thrust-kick (N)]-[leg-forward front-stance (N) counter-down-block (NE/NW)]-[drive-in front-stance (NE/NW) counter-punch].

Exercise IIB-42

Apply Exercise IIB-41 in sparring:
[A: [punch]-[block]-[kick]]&[D: [block]-[kick]-[punch]].
[A: [kick]-[block]-[punch]]&[D: [block]-[punch]-[kick]].
Then A has the choice of which combination to initiate, and D attempts to react with the correct strategy.

Final Exercise

[Combination]. [Meditate]. [Bow].

b. First Exercise

[Meditate]. [Bow]. [Warm-up]. [Kata].

Exercise IIB-43

[Step-back back-stance outside-round-block]-[front-snap-kick]-[punch].
[Step-in up-block]-[counter-punch]-[front-thrust-kick].
[Step-in strike-snap]-[counter-inside-round-block]-[side-thrust-kick].
[Front-leg side-snap-kick (N)]-[down-block (N)]-[step-in punch (N)].

Exercise IIB-44

Apply Exercise IIB-43 in sparring, similar to Exercise IIB-42.

Final Exercise

[Combination]. [Meditate]. [Bow].

c. First Exercise

[Meditate]. [Bow]. [Warm-up]. [Kata].

Exercise IIB-45

[Step-back side-stance (W) inside-round-block (N) face]-[side-snap-kick (N)]-[step-in punch (N)].
[Step-in back-stance knife-hand-block]-[counter-punch]-[front-thrust-kick].
[Step-in strike-snap]-[step-back outside-round-block]-[front-snap-kick].
[Front-leg side-thrust-kick (W/E)]-[down-block (W/E)]-[step-in punch (W/E)].

Exercise IIB-46

Apply Exercise IIB-45 in sparring, similar to Exercise IIB-42.

Final Exercise

[Combination]. [Meditate]. [Bow].

IIB-8. Sparring at Different Distances

This week's training stresses the different qualities of body and attention techniques needed at different distances from an opponent.

In general, at close distances, there is hardly enough time for simple reactions. One should use body feeling to continually either drive through the center of an opponent or work around to attack the sides or back.

At medium distances, just barely within [counter-punch] range, it is possible and wise to use rhythmic body combinations as a strategy. A whole arsenal of techniques becomes available.

At long distances, roughly equal or greater than one and a half techniques distance (measured in time of [counter-punch] units), typically only simple direct techniques have a chance at all of succeeding. The strategy necessarily depends on closing the distance effectively, by the use of [feints] and [shifting], until medium- or short-distance techniques can be used.

a. First Exercise

[Meditate]. [Bow]. [Warm-up]. [Kata].

Exercise IIB-47

Prepare a 4 or 5 step close-distance [combination], using the [elbows] and [knees]. Use the guidelines of Section IIB-7 to create an effective combination.

Exercise IIB-48

Apply Exercise IIB-47:
[A: [step-in punch]-[slide-in]-[* several short-distance-techniques]]
&[D: [step-back block]-[slide-in]-[* several short-distance-techniques]].

Exercise IIB-49

Prepare a 4 or 5 step medium-distance [combination].

Exercise IIB-50

Apply Exercise IIB-49:
[A: [step-in-punch]-[* several medium-distance-techniques]]
&[D: [step-back block]-[* several medium-distance-techniques]].

Exercise IIB-51

Prepare a 4 or 5 step long-distance combination with sliding and stretched techniques.

Exercise IIB-52

Apply Exercise IIB-51:
[A: [step-in punch]-[step-back]-[* step-in with several techniques]]
&[D: [step-back block]-[step-back]-[* step-in with several techniques]].

Final Exercise

[Combination]. [Meditate]. [Bow].

b. First Exercise

[Meditate]. [Bow]. [Warm-up]. [Kata].

Exercise IIB-53

Do Exercises IIB-47-48-49-50-51-52.

Exercise IIB-54

Combine Exercises IIB-48-50-52: Each side commits himself or herself to a specific distance-strategy. When rotating to a new opponent, he or she must again pick a specific distance-strategy, but not the one picked just previously.

Final Exercise

[Combination]. [Meditate]. [Bow].

c. First Exercise

[Meditate]. [Bow]. [Warm-up]. [Kata].

Exercise IIB-55

Do Exercises IIB-53-54.

Final Exercise

[Combination]. [Meditate]. [Bow].

IIB-9. Attention and Sparring

Specific attentional skills must be trained just as specific body skills must be trained. The main point of this week's practice is to develop clean perception-to-technique reactions.

a. First Exercise

[Meditate]. [Bow]. [Warm-up]. [Kata].

Exercise IIB-56

This series of exercises develops eye-to-body coordination. They are based on the premise that most people react more instinctively when they feel some tactile stimulus, rather than their typically slower and more complex reactions when they only see the same stimulus.

Both sides start as usual in [front-stance (L)] facing each other. Do each of the following A&D sequences repeatedly across the floor before interchanging A and D:
[A: (#1) [counter-punch face/stomach/groin]
&[D: [touch opponent's would-be counter-punch-hand]-[(#1) counter-sweep-block]].

[A: (#1) [step-in punch face/stomach/groin]/[front-thrust-kick]]
&[D: [touch opponent's would-be punch-hand]-[(#1) step-back sweep-block]].

[A: (#1) [step-in punch face/stomach/groin]/[[front-thrust-kick]]
&[D: [touch opponent's would-be pulling-hand]-[(#1) step-back sweep-block]].

[A: [step-in punch]/[front-thrust-kick]]
&[D: [step-back block]].

Final Exercise

[Combination]. [Meditate]. [Bow].

b. First Exercise

[Meditate]. [Bow]. [Warm-up]. [Kata].

Exercise IIB-57

Do Exercise IIB-56

Exercise IIB-58

Have students react sharply to the command [punch]. Then again to the command [kick]. Then give three commands at a time, and have students quickly react with three full [step-in] movements, executing the required sequence:
[Punch]/[kick]-[punch]/[kick]-[punch]/[kick].

Exercise IIB-59

Do Exercise IC-3 from PART I, trying to [D: counter-punch] as a reaction to a [A: counter-punch].

Exercise IIB-60

In this exercise, after an initial interaction, both sides may either [counter-attack (R)] with their right side, or [block (L)] with their left side and then [counter-attack (R)]. The idea is to win, not lose, so if both sides [A: attack]&[D: attack] at the same time, both sides lose. If a [block] is unsuccessful, the student must not attempt [counter-attack], but rather admit defeat. Both sides start in [front-stance (R)].

The initial engagement is:
[A: [step-in punch (L)] stomach]]
&[D: [step-back outside-round-block (L)]].
Then, either side can immediately attempt to [attack]:
[A: [counter-punch (R) face/stomach]]
&[D: [up-block (L)/down-block (L)]-[counter-punch (R)]]].

Final Exercise

[Combination]. [Meditate]. [Bow].

c. First Exercise

[Meditate]. [Bow]. [Warm-up]. [Kata].

Exercise IIB-61

Do Exercises IIB-56-59-60.

Exercise IIB-62

Add [front-thrust-kick] to Exercise IIB-60: After the initial engagement, either side can also attempt a third alternative to [A: [counter-punch (R) face/stomach]]:
[A: [front-thrust-kick (R) stomach]]
&[D: [side-shift down-block (L)]-[counter-punch (R)].

Final Exercise

[Combination]. [Meditate]. [Bow].

IIB-10. Feints

There are several ways to break an opponent's balance. You can do this physically with a [throw]/[sweep]/[attack]/[attack-block]. You can also break an opponent's attention by raising his or her emotional state to the level where most of his or her attention is diverted or distorted by this emotion. However, against a strong, worthy opponent who is paying careful attention to your every move, the most crucial part of the engagement is to prepare for the actual physical interaction. This is done by first attempting to break his or her attention for a fraction of a second. Of course, the only effective way of performing this is to possess body technique trained to the level that you can emit an "aura" of an intended technique of [move] or [pause] to your opponent. Your opponent then may react to this intended technique with his or her full body commitment, a [block]/[shift]/[counter-attack]. However, you do not commit yourself fully to your projected intended technique, but rather pursue a different pre-planned strategy against your opponent.

For intermediate students, who typically do not possess the level of trained technique described above, practicing [feints] can be accomplished simply by having them equate a [feint] with an [attack] that is focussed half-way between their own hip-center and the intended target. For advanced students, [feint] will be equated with a more subtle [movement]-[transition] into the intended strategy.

a. First Exercise

[Meditate]. [Bow]. [Warm-up]. [Kata].

Exercise IIB-63

A basic exercise can convey the typical [feint] feeling of "rippling" off several body techniques from one main body [movement]:

First, establish the main body [movement]:
[Step-in punch].

Then, try to distract the opponent's attention, covering the often telling jerky beginning motion of the technique: Keep the [stance] and [hip-movement] the same, but let the initial [hip-movement] automatically throw off the forward hand, without attempting a follow-up body focus, under the line of sight of the opponent:
[Short-punch no focus]-[step-in punch].

Next, focus a technique just about as the feet cross while in forward motion:
[Short-punch no focus]-[as-feet-cross punch]-[counter-punch].

Finally, add in a [kick]:
[Short-punch no focus]-[before-feet-cross punch]-[front-snap-kick]-[counter-punch].

In the last two sequences, the middle techniques are the [feints], and the end [counter-punch] is the strategically preplanned final [attack].

Exercise IIB-64

Try [feints] in sparring:
[A: [[punch]-[punch]]/[[feint-punch]-[punch]]]
&[D: [[block]-[punch]]/[punch]].
The attacker A follows up the option [feint-punch] with a [punch], in case D does not immediately fill in this space with [D: punch].

Final Exercise

[Combination]. [Meditate]. [Bow].

b. First Exercise

[Meditate]. [Bow]. [Warm-up]. [Kata].

Exercise IIB-65

Do Exercises IIB-63-64.

Exercise IIB-66

Use the [feint-punch] to create an opening for [kick]:
[A: [[punch]-[punch]-[kick]]/[[feint-punch]-[punch]-[kick]]]
&[D: [[block]-[block]-[counter-punch]]/[[punch]-[block]-[counter-punch]]].

Final Exercise

[Combination]. [Meditate]. [Bow].

c. First Exercise

[Meditate]. [Bow]. [Warm-up]. [Kata].

Exercise IIB-67

Do Exercises IIB-63-64-65.

Exercise IIB-68

Use [feint-knee-kick]:
[A: [[kick]-[punch]-[kick]/[punch]]/[[feint-knee-kick]-[punch]-[kick]/[punch]]]
&[D: [[block]-[block]-[counter-punch]]/[[punch]-[block]-[counter-punch]]]].

Final Exercise

[Combination]. [Mediate]. [Bow].

IIB-11. Combinations in Sparring

This week's practice permits students to try out new feelings/strategies learned in the previous ten weeks.

a,b,c. First Exercise

[Meditate]. [Bow]. [Warm-up]. [Kata]. [Combination 1].

Exercise IIB-69

The attacker prepares a 5 to 6 step [attack-combination], a new one for each new opponent.

Exercise IIB-70

The attacker does the [combination] quickly, while the defender [moves-back] just out of touching range of all techniques. Do several times.

Exercise IIB-71

The attacker slows down the [combination] a bit. The defender now develops a defense strategy to [block] each and every [attack]. The defender does not counter-attack. Do several times.

Exercise IIB-72

The defender attempts to [counter-attack] to stop the [A: attack-combination]. Each attacker becomes a referee for his or her engagement, and stops the [attack] only if timing, distance and technique of the defender's [D: counter-attack] are all accept-able. Do several times.

Exercise IIB-73

The attacker modifies the original [attack-combination], with respect to timing, distance or technique. Repeat Exercise IIB-72.

Exercise IIB-74

The attacker slowly attempts to create an [attack-combination] while the defender moves back but slowly [D: * counter-attacks] to show the attacker where D perceives flaws in A's [combination]. Do several times until the attacker has created an [attack-combination] specific to his or her opponent. Repeat Exercises IIB-71-72.

Final Exercise

[Combination 2]. [Meditate]. [Bow].

IIB-12. Improvisation, Review

Especially after the freedom of technique exercised the previous week, students must come back to hone their techniques in preparation for the exam next week.

a,b,c. First Exercise

[Meditate]. [Bow]. [Warm-up].

Exercise IIB-75

Practice [kata] with physical themes such as stance, momentum between techniques, body expansion and compression between techniques, focusing on targets, etc.

Practice [kata] with attentional themes such as increased concentration on focus of technique, awareness of opponent especially between techniques, attentional rhythms specific to each kata, etc., as discussed in Section IC-3.

Exercise IIB-76

Do [improvisation], Exercise IC-22. Colored belts should be graded on this exercise, perhaps to count as part of their exam next week.

Exercise IIB-77

[Spar] according to the level required in the exam.

Final Exercise

[Combination]. [Meditate]. [Bow].

The written exam is given out as a "take-home" exam, to be opened and taken during one hour selected by the student. At the time of the physical exam, students who have not disciplined themselves to take this exam on their own will take their written exam while the other students perform their physical exams.

IIB-13. Kyu and Dan Exams

First, an analogy between karate belt levels and academic school levels will help to clarify the meaning of "levels." I consider a Black Belt to roughly correspond to a Bachelor's degree. In any college, some undergraduates are smarter or quicker than some graduate students. However, a good faculty member appreciates that an average graduate student has more academic maturity than an average undergraduate student. A graduate student may have been a "B" undergraduate student, but the "A" undergraduate student is still an undergraduate. The only objective way to run a school is to test for specific skills at each level, as defined by a peer group of faculty members. Some beginners may have more talent than some advanced students, but until that talent is specifically tested, that student must pass each test at the standardized levels. Finally, at Black Belt level, a set of basic skills have been tested, and a given student may pass at a "C", "B" or "A" level. When a student under 16 years old first passes a Black Belt exam, it is considered a 1 Dan Jr. Black Belt grade, because although the correct dynamics are present, usually power and sparring maturity are not. He or she continues to take the Black Belt exam every six months until the level is clearly the same as the adult Black Belt.

Second, the exam is an objective class experience for all students, and they learn to appreciate what is required at other levels as well. Since many students are nervous at karate exams, this is also a small "moment of truth" for them. They must perform, ready or not, under stressful conditions, exactly how they should be training in all their classes!

Black Belts, as part of their ongoing training, should sit up front with the examining instructor, and commit their own judgements on students to writing, to be discussed later with the examining instructor. Black Belts typically take their physical exam twice a year, instead of four times a year. They are also graded on the quality of questions they submit to be considered for use on the written kyu exam.

A couple of sample written tests, and a rather complete set of physical kyu and dan exams follow. Remember, for colored belts, Exercise IIB-76 is also a reasonable contribution to their final grade.

Written Kyu Test 1

I.

    (A) Explain the "kinematics" of [punching]: Describe how power is developed for a [punch] from: (1) [side-stance]; (2) [front-stance counter-punch]; (3) [step-in punch].

    (B) Explain the "body dynamics" of continuous [punching]: Describe how power is maintained and controlled *between* two [punches]: (1) in [side-stance]; (2) during [punch]-[counter-punch]; (3) during [step-in punch]-[step-in punch].

    (C) Explain the "attention dynamics" of continuous [punching] during [sparring]: Describe the (1) *purpose* (the point of charging with a strategy of [punch]-[punch], (2) *risk* (what might you expect your opponent to do between your two punches), and (3) *alternatives* (what should you be prepared to do if your opponent executes the strategy described in I(C)(2)).

II.

    (A) Explain the kinematics of [front-snap-kick].

    (B) Explain the body dynamics connecting [front-snap-kick] and any other specific [kick].

    (C) Explain the attention dynamics of continuous [kicking]: Describe the (1) *purpose*, (2) *risk*, and (3) *alternatives*.

III.

    (A) Explain the kinematics of [front-thrust-kick].

    Explain the body dynamics connecting [front-thrust-kick] and a [punch].

    (C) Explain the attention dynamics of continuous (any) [kick] followed by any [hand-attack]: Describe the (1) *purpose*, (2) *risk*, and (3) *alternatives*.

Written Kyu Test 2

    Pick which Strategy below is correct (best). Explicitly show why the other Strategies are inferior by stating which of the Emotion-Attention Cycles each violates:

Strategies

    FIRST. Withdraw from several aggressive attacks until a [pause] is perceived, then [counter-attack].

    SECOND. Heap a flurry of [attacks] on your opponent, confusing him or her, then [pause], wait for an [attack] from your opponent, and [counter-attack].

    THIRD. [Attack] fists and feet of your opponent, antagonizing him or her. When the opponent is at the peak of anger, [attack].

Emotion-Attention Cycles

   A. Fear usually causes a conflict (and arousal) between focused and global attention.

   B. Anxiety is usually accompanied by a loss of focused and global attentions.

   C. Anger usually narrows focused attention.

   D. As anger dissipates, focused attention usually becomes weaker, and global
attention turns inwards.

   E. The optimum emotional state for [sparring] causes sufficient arousal to
integrate focused and global attention to bear on the specific engagement.

Answers

   The FIRST strategy is most correct by D.

   The SECOND strategy is not as good by B. When confusion (anxiety) is sensed
in the opponent, don't pause, [attack].

   The THIRD strategy is incorrect by C. You will probably find yourself [attacking]
simultaneously with your opponent's [attack]. Both of you will lose.

Physical Exams

8 Kyu -- White Belt

Look for: balance and sense of stance, punching, kicking.
Kata: [Heian #1].

Basics:
8a: [step-in punch].
8b: [step-back up-block].
8c: [step-in outside-round-block].
8d: [step-back back-stance knife-hand-block].
8e: [front-snap-kick].
8f: [stepping-across-side-stance side-snap/thrust-kick].

Spar: [A: [step-in punch (R) face],[step-in punch face],[step-in punch face]]
&[D: [step-back up-block (L)],[step-back up-block],[step-back up-block]-[counter-
punch]].
Instructor counts for each attack.

7 Kyu

Look for: better balance in combinations.

Kata: [Heian #2].

Basics:
7a = 8a.
7b: [step-back up-block],[counter-punch].
7c: [step-in outside-round-block],[counter-punch].
7d = 8d.
7e = 8e.
7f: [round-snap-kick].
7g = 8f.

Spar: [three-step-spar] similar to 8 Kyu, but [attack stomach], no count.

6 Kyu -- Green Belt

Look for: use of stance and hips, sense of body expansion and compression.

Kata: [Heian #3].

Basics:
6a = 7a.
6b = 7b.
6c: [step-in outside-round-block (N)],[side-stance (W/E) reverse-rotation elbow-strike (N)].
6d = 7d-[front-leg front-snap-kick].
6e: [front-snap-kick (L/R)]-[front-snap-kick (R/L)].
6f: [round-kick].
6g = 7g.
6h: [front-snap-kick]-[punch].

Spar: [A: [! step-in punch face]]&[D: [block]-[! counter-punch]].
[A: [! step-in punch stomach]]&[D: [block]-[! counter-punch]].

5 Kyu

Look for: better use of stance and hips.

Kata: [Heian #4].

Basics:
5a = 6a.
5b = 6b.
5c = 6c-[strike-snap (N) face].
5d = 6d-[counter-spear-hand-punch].
5e: [front-snap-kick (R/L)]-[round-snap-kick (L/R)]-[counter-punch (R/L)].
5f: [round-snap-kick (L/R) stomach]-[round-snap-kick (R/L) face].
5g = 6g.
5h = 6h.

Spar: Add to 6 Kyu [A: [! front-thrust-kick]]&[D: [block]-[! counter-punch]].

4 Kyu

Look for: better sense of body expansion and compression, sense of dynamics between techniques.

Kata: [Heian #5].

Basics:
4a = 5a.
4b = 5b.
4c = 5c.
4d = 5d.
4e = 5e-[down-block].
4f: [front-snap-kick (L/R,N)]-[side-thrust-kick (R/L,N)]-[counter-punch (L/R)]-[down-block].
4g = 5g.
4h = 5h.

Spar: Add to 5 Kyu [A: [! side-thrust-kick]]&[D: [block]-[! counter-punch]].

3 Kyu -- Brown Belt

Look for: use of body expansion and compression, sense of dynamics.

Kata: [Tekki #1].

Basics: On Brown and Black Belt exams, start in [free-stance] and do three sets each of the basics:

3a = 4a.

3b: [step-in back-stance knife-hand-block]-[front-leg front-snap-kick]-[counter-punch].

3c: [front-snap-kick (R/L)]-[round-snap-kick (L/R)]-[counter-punch (R/L)]-[strike-snap].

3d: [round-snap-kick (R/L)]-[side-thrust-kick (L/R)]-[counter-knife-hand-strike-lock (R/L)]-[strike-snap].

3e: [counter-punch]-[round-snap-kick (R/L)]-[side-thrust-kick (R/L)]-[counter-knife-hand-strike-lock (L/R)]-[strike-snap].

3f: [step-back up-block]-[front-snap-kick]-[punch].

3g: [focus punch on moving-pencil-eraser].

Spar: same as 4 Kyu.

2 Kyu

Look for: better use of dynamics:

Kata: pick [independent form].

Basics:

2a = 3a.

2b: [step-in-punch], [step-in-punch]-[step-in-punch].

2c = 3b.

2d = 3d.

2e = 3e.

2f: [round-snap-kick (R/L)]-[side-thrust-kick (R/L)]-[step-in punch (L/R)].

2g = 3f.

2h = 3g.

Spar: same as 3 Kyu.

1 Kyu

Look for: proficient use of dynamics.

Kata: different [independent form] than 2 Kyu.

Basics:
1a = 2a.
1b = 2b.
1c = 2c.
1d = 2d.
1e = 2e.
1f = 2f.
1g = 2g.
1h: [step-back outside-round-block (R/L)]-[punch (R/L)]-[front-leg front-snap-kick]-[counter-punch].
1i = 2h.

Spar: same as 2 Kyu.

1 Dan -- Black Belt

Look for: proficient use of dynamics in all techniques, sense of timing.

Kata: different [independent form] than Kyu exams.

Basics:
1A = 1b.
1B: [step-in back-stance knife-hand-block]-[front-leg front-snap-kick (R/L)]-[leg-back]-[back-stance (L) knife-hand-block]-[step-in punch].
1C = 1d.
1D = [round-snap-kick (R/L)]-[side-snap-kick (L/R)]-[step-in punch (R/L)].
1E = 1g.
1F = 1h.
1G = 1i.
1H: 8 to 10 step [combination] prepared for the exam.
1I: Exercise IC-13 against two opponents.

Spar: similar to 1 Kyu, but A and D in [free-stance] and using [feints].

2 Dan

Look for: use of dynamics in sparring, better timing.

Kata: different [independent form] than in previous exams.
Quiz on selected techniques from [kata].

Basics:
2A = 1B.
2B = 1C.
2C = 1D.
2D = 1F.
2E = 1G.
2F: Exercise IC-13 against three opponents.

Spar: Same as 1 Dan.
[Free-spar] against two (separate) opponents.

3 Dan

Look for: use of dynamics and timing in sparring.

Kata: different [independent form] than previous exams.
Quiz on selected techniques in [kata].

Basics:
3A: Create and perform three 8 to 10 step [combinations] to selected themes.
3B = 2G.

Spar: [Free-spar] against three (separate) opponents.

Thesis: Write and defend an original thesis on karate.

4 Dan

Depends on school. Usually several [kata] are required to be performed, and [free-sparring] similar to 3 Dan. Another thesis is required.

5 Dan +

5th Dan and higher also require original contributions, but the thesis as well as service done for the school are counted. These higher level belts are usually considered honorary administrative titles.

IIB-14. Self-Defense

This class should be taught as an exercise in decision-making. This helps to keep a person cool under impending danger, and permits him or her to exert some control over the situation. Afterwards, this also minimizes anxiety, guilt or shame, independent of the outcome. Keep all decisions simple with a few alternatives.

Decision 1

Keep an open global attention to the situation. If at all possible, talk first to explore all possibilties and escapes. Don't be passive. Don't be nasty. Be firm and to the point. For example: "Don't do that!" "Stop that!" "Leave me alone!"

Decision 2

If force is obviously required, you must decide whether to [surprise-attack] or to [counter-attack] just after your assailant first [attacks] you. Be prepared to get hurt, as well as to fully commit yourself to the attack. Use techniques that promote the full use of the body and that are effective against heavy targets.

Decision 3

Concentrate on the attack:
Target: [eyes]/[throat]/[groin]/[side-of-knee]/[instep].
Technique: [bear-claw-thrust]/[palm-thrust]/[elbow-strike]/[knee-kick]/[heel-stomp].
Follow-up is essential. Repeatedly [attack] for as long as you remain within range of any targets.

Decision 4

Move away to examine the situation. Come back to global attention. [Attack] again? Call for help? Run away?

Decision 5

Report incident to authorities. This is hardly a decision. You must protect yourself as well as other potential victims. You must report injuries or deaths.

The class can take the following structure:

Exercise IIB-78

[Warm-up]. As this class may be for people only interested in self-defense, only for one or a few class sessions, other ceremonies are meaningless. The point of true karate training, and its necessity for proper technique, has already been made in the required introductory class, Section IIA-0.

Exercise IIB-79

Practice all techniques in Decision 3 individually on a hitting bag.

Exercise IIB-80

Practice doing [combinations] of 3 to 5 techniques in Decision 3 on the hitting bag.

Exercise IIB-81

Do exercises similar to IC-13-14, but have the attackers holding hitting bags as targets.

Exercise IIB-82

Practice Exercises IIB-79-81 after breaking away from grabs.

A useful reference for self-defense is:
F. Demura and D. Ivan, *Street Survival* (Japan Publications, Tokyo, 1979).

IIB-15. T'ai Chi
Stick-Sparring

An excellent complementary training to karate is t'ai chi. A separate class, or a quarterly workshop can be devoted to learning t'ai chi form(s). Some book references are given at the end of Chapter IC.

I have developed a particularly useful training for novices as well as expert karate students, akin to [pushing hands], a t'ai chi form of sparring training. The idea is to teach students to fluidly move and shift, to seek weak balance and positions of opponents, from which they may then initiate a strong [attack]. The stick is held by both opponents and acts like a filter of information flowing between them, like the neck of an hour-glass. Both sides feed bits of information through this neck, filtering complex body activity into a few basic physical feelings that directly relate to the basic principles in PART I.

Exercise IIB-83

THRUSTING. Some preliminary exercises are necessary to develop the "ground rules." Use a stick about 30 inches long, for example, cut from an old broom. Each side holds the stick just tightly enough to support its weight, but freely enough to slide along it, even to exchange hand positions. Both sides start in [free-stance] holding the stick, each person holding it near both ends. The most natural position has the leading hand the same as the leading leg.
[A: * [step-in thrust]]&[D: * [step-back]].
The defense should match the beginning and end of the attack's movement. Both sides finish in relaxed [free-stance].

Figure IIB-83. [Stick-sparring] starting position.

Exercise IIB-84

STRIKING. [A: * [step-in circling]]&[D: * [circle/side-shift away]]. The attacker should make large circles emanating from the hip-center, with the arms and legs forming extensions of these simple curved movements. Again, both sides finish in [free-stance].

Exercise IIB-85

BODY EXPANSION-COMPRESSION. The attacker starts any [* thrusting] or [* striking] technique. The defender goes with this movement until just near its completion, permitting his or her body to be somewhat stretched or compressed by the final movement of the attack. The defender uses this "spring energy" to initiate a [* step-in counter-thrust]/[* step-in counter-strike] just at the end of this interaction.

Exercise IIB-86

[* Stick-sparring] is a continuous interaction of movements like Exercise IIB-85. Never pull or push along the line or curve of power being created by your opponent. The stick always moves, at a constant slow speed, in the compromise trajectory defined by the resultant forces imparted on it from both people. Keep moving constantly and smoothly, finding transitions between techniques and angles of shifting to set up your opponent for [counter-attacks]. At each imminent transition, attempt to capture the leadership into the next movement.

Since you both are moving slowly and smoothly, and not competing with direct opposing force, it is unlikely that you will often win, "stabbing" or "cutting" with the stick. Instead, you are practicing preparatory moves to complement your regular karate training.

Figure IIB-86a. The start of [stick-sparring] where the defender has started to [circle-shift] away from an [overhead-strike].

Figure IIB-86b. The defender is [circle-shifting] away from an [overhead-strike].

Figure IIB-86c. The defender has [circle-shifted] away from an [overhead-strike].

Figure IIB-86d. The start of [stick-sparring], with a different striking angle from the previous three illustrations, where the defender starts to [shift-back] away from an [underhand-strike].

Figure IIB-86e. The defender is [shifting-back]&[circle-shifting] away from an [underhand-strike].

Figure IIB-86f. The defender has [shifted] away from an [underhand-strike].

IIC. Advanced Dynamics

This chapter presents an outline of a free-sparring class. It is assumed that all the students have just previously warmed up and practiced in a rigorous class, such as one of the intermediate classes described in Chapter IIB.

Exercise IIC-1

[Meditate]. [Bow].

Exercise IIC-2

Students must practice control if they are to learn to spar hard and fast, touching targets instead of hitting or missing them. They should not have to rely on armor or protection of any kind. They should all practice to do correctly focused techniques. Indeed, maximum power requires the combination of speed and mass possible only with correctly focused techniques.

This exercise reinforces this attitude. Students line up by a bar or wall and practice focusing techniques close to, but not touching this solid target. For this practice, consider this bar or wall as being north of the practice room. A "+" will signify that a technique [... +] is to be focused on the bar or wall. Each string of techniques starts and ends in [free-stance]. In these exercises the students must step back to the starting position after each sequence, wipe their minds clear of the previous techniques, and start again. Try a few sets of 10 on each side, each set requiring a kiai [!...] on a specific technique.

[Counter-punch +].

[Front-thrust-kick +].

[Strike-snap]-[side-thrust-kick +]-[counter-punch +].

[Front-thrust-kick +]-[counter-punch +].

[Front-stance (W/E)]-[side-thrust-kick +]-[strike-snap +]-[counter-punch +]-[front-stance (W/E)].

[Counter-punch (S)]-[back-thrust-kick +]-[counter-punch +]-[turn (S)]-[front-stance (S)].

[Front-snap-kick +]-[punch +].

[Front-snap-kick +]-[counter-punch +]-[bottom-fist-strike-lock +].

[Counter-punch]-[round-snap-kick +]-[counter-punch +].

[Slide-back up-block]-[slide-forward counter-punch]-[front-thrust-kick +].

[Adjust-distance back-stance palm-punch +]-[adjust-distance counter-punch +]-[adjust-distance front-knee-kick +].

[Slide-back back-stance (W/E) strike-snap (W/E)]-[side-snap-kick +]-[counter-punch +].

[Circle-shift outside-round-block (W/E)]-[round-snap-kick +]-[counter-punch +].

Exercise IIC-3

This is a good place to insert some timing exercises, such as a two-person-combination, Exercise IC-16. Another possibility is for one student to stand with his or her back to the wall, and spar with specific techniques with a student who is charging from a line of other students.

Exercise IIC-4

CONTINUOUS-TWO-PERSON-COMBINATION. This is a good warm-up for [free-sparring], and also trains students to develop good sparring habits. Students spar strong and fast with each other using specific techniques. Distance is important, and they should be instructed to take extra steps, if necessary, before each attack, in order that they have a realistic chance of touching their target. After each sequence, the initial attack and defense sides quickly switch techniques, and they continue alternating in this fashion until the instructor stops the exercise. A few examples are:
[A: [punch face]-[punch stomach]]/[[punch stomach]-[punch face]]]
&[D: [block]-[block]].

[A: [front-thrust-kick]-[punch]]
&[D: [lateral-shift block]-[lateral-shift block]].

[A: [punch]-[front-thrust-kick]]
&[D: [lateral-shift block]-[lateral-shift block]].

[A: [[punch]-[thrust-kick]]/[[thrust-kick]-[punch]]]
&[D: [lateral-shift block]-[lateral-shift block]].

[A: [punch]-[block]-[kick]]
&[D: [block]-[kick]-[block]].

[A: [punch]-[kick]]
&[D: [block]-[block]].

[A: [[punch]-[kick]]/[[kick]-[punch]]]
&[D: [block]-[block]].

[A: [punch]-[punch]/[kick]]
&[D: [block]-[counter-punch]].

[A: [punch]/[feint-punch]-[punch]/[kick]]
&[D: [block]/[move-in]-[counter-punch]].

Exercise IIC-5

Break the class into two groups for fast and slow [free-sparring]. The instructor must decide who belongs to each group. Students within each group spar with each other for 5-minute periods.

Exercise IIC-6

Teach a new [kata]. Then each student practices his or her current [kata], to generalize and apply new feelings from the new [kata].

Exercise IIC-7

Final exercises that build strength and endurance also prevent accidents due to sloppily performed techniques:
[Push-ups] on knuckles.
[Squat]-[kick] repeatedly.
[Punching] in "jack-knife" position on floor.
From [counter-punch] position: [[punch]&[front-snap-kick]]-[! [leg-back]&[counter-punch]].

Exercise IIC-8

[Meditate]. [Bow].

Exercise IIC-9

All students [punch] and [kick] against bags and boards.

PART III. LIVING DYNAMICS

IIIA. Beyond Class

The following is a write-up of an invited lecture I gave to a UC San Diego "Frontiers of Science" seminar on 15 January 1980. Bernd Matthias, a popular physicist, ran the course for several years, and I was a regularly invited lecturer to his seminar. In October of 1980, Bernd died of a heart attack. He was a dear friend and colleague of mine for twenty years, and although we had quite different interests, we shared many common social, scientific, and some not-so-scientific perceptions of reality.

I have put this lecture in this book because I believe it gives an important context to training in karate, or to training in any specialized discipline that advertises individual and societal growth in its practitioners.

There is also a more direct reason for appreciating how a specialized training fits into other possible aspects of your life. I don't believe in ultimate justice -- there are too many counter-examples in the world around us. However, I do believe that you will become better at whatever you do, if you are a wiser and stronger person in body, mind and spirit. If you can realize even a small amount of some real and testable similarities in the dynamics of your art with the rest of your life, then you will find that instead of training in your art only a few hours a week, you will be essentially practicing your art every moment. Practice may not make perfect, but it does make better, and you need to practice as much as possible. Furthermore, you will be able to bring to bear powerful tools from your art to apply to other facets of life. This complimentary interaction between your practice and the rest of life should eventually merge with you standing tall as a steady, healthy individual interacting with our biophysical universe.

IIIB. "Consciousness -- Physics or Metaphysics?"

Introduction

Last week you heard Bernd Matthias explain the genius of such men as Kepler and Pauli as being derived not only from their superior intellectual abilities, but also from their insight to appreciate the philosophical and metaphysical context of the world around them. Today, our understanding of the phenomenon of gravity is relatively quite advanced beyond Kepler's concepts. Thus, we too often tend to devalue the mystical non-scientific beliefs and processes by which Kepler the human evolved his ideas, in favor of lauding him for his three still-standing scientific laws of planetary motion.

Today I will use similar arguments to discuss the phenomenon of consciousness, a concept by no means clearly analytically developed. At best, we are at the stage of Kepler with regard to our understanding of this phenomenon, and so it is quite relevant to take stock of our investigative tools. In some ways, consciousness is the ultimate phenomenon -- the process by which we investigate other processes.

Recently I have developed an analytic model of macroscopic brain functioning that may describe some aspects of consciousness, e.g. attention and self-awareness. I will slant my discussion of consciousness to examine what and from where arise investigative tools necessary to develop any such understanding of these phenomena. My basic theme is that a true understanding, similar to just about any true investigation of nature, requires a testable analysis guided by good insight based on valid data. A sprinkling of decent and moral motivations doesn't hurt, and a willingness to look for specific projects to advance applications to everyday life may be more than relevant -- they may be essential!

We all have our particular sense of what we consider consciousness to be, or what we feel it should be. It is useful to list a few desirable attributes of any process of investigation that, on one hand, is general enough to satisfy most of us, and on the other hand, is specific enough to directly contribute to any enlightening investigation. These contributing attributes are: spiritual purpose, intuitive insight, objective data, analytic paradigm, and personal/societal application. I sense that much confusion and disagreement about consciousness stems from the conscious or unconscious lack of communication among people who give more or less weight to these different attributes.

The very disciplines that are best designed to use these attributes of investigation are themselves rather mutually exclusive. For example, among many disciplines that contribute to our quest for knowledge, there are: old and new religions, axiomatic metaphysical mind/body disciplines, neurosciences, physics, and scientifically applied disciplines of the biological, social and natural sciences.

In the context of my model of consciousness, I suggest that the above disciplines rather excel in contributing a particular attribute. I also suggest that each of these disciplines and their "expert" disciples are relatively poor in the other attributes. The list of positive correlations, between disciplines and the attributes in which they excel, are:

Old & New Religions: Spiritual Purpose
Metaphysical Mind/Body Disciplines: Intuitive Insight
Neuroscience: Objective Data
Physics: Analytic Paradigm
Applied Sciences: Personal/Societal Application

You might even expand this list to demonstrate that each discipline is relatively poor in even more attributes! However, a wiser way of viewing this situation is to realize that all these disciplines, especially at this stage of our knowledge, are essential in order that any process of investigation be most fruitful. This list of correlations is largely made possible by the narrow, often bigoted experts of each discipline who refuse to or cannot comprehend the essence of the other disciplines. They have all forged their clear but schizophrenic view of the universe. Today, as in no other previous era, civilization is advanced enough to appreciate all these attributes. Hopefully, the individual members of this civilization will also advance to this same realization.

We should not confuse the strengths and weaknesses of these disciplines, nor should we forget that they are all essential to investigate consciousness. For example, even assuming that much of consciousness can eventually be objectified and codified, e.g. by neuroscientists and physicists, the essence of the process of investigation, consciousness, into new frontiers will remain the same. The religious and metaphysical systems of today that motivate and help us to forge intuitive insights capable of being processed by our minds, may become the archaic systems and crutches of the past. But these systems are our slaves, and not vice versa. We should be flexible enough to eventually discard well-used and antiquated structures, but open enough to accept those required by our present world. Everything changes except the process! Perhaps the awareness of this process of consciousness may be sufficient to make us wise enough to know when to change to new systems and structures, and to which of them we owe our gratitude.

Today, I'd like to discuss the processes by which I perceive some solutions to some perplexing concepts of consciousness.

Spiritual Purpose

During my 7 pre-teen years in an orthodox Hebrew school, I acquired the notion that God -- what I now conceive of as the deanthropomorphized universe -- imparts a natural, not necessarily rational, order to all things; and that we humans can achieve an understanding of this natural order, and even exert a partial control of our environment without too badly upsetting it, if we apply other humanly natural concepts of morality and justice. I also acquired the notion that it is noble to use this gain to help others to live and love in a better world.

Remarkably, these notions were still prevalent during the 1960's, even in the universities! Of course, we all now know that the 1970's changed most of that and that today's Golden Rule is: "He who has the gold makes the rules." However, I still believe in these old notions, and I hope the 1980's restores some of them. Perhaps new gains in our understanding of our consciousness, more than any other technological achievement of the 1980's may help to bring peace to our planet. Consciousness is more than an area of research or selfish self-development. It is much too important to leave to any one group of experts to study!

The spiritual zeal to contribute to an abstract divine being or to a body of knowledge is among the strongest of our cerebral sources of motivation and drives. When sufficiently strong, it can guide or overcome more primitive midbrain centers of desires and drives. Without such zeal to help us to persevere, much scientific and technological innovation just simply would not have favorable statistical odds of occurring. Of course, most people in all professions still work primarily for concrete cash or for glorious rewards, but history testifies to the important contributions made by spiritual societies and individual spiritual zealots such as Kepler.

Intuitive Insights

Over 22 years ago I first developed one of my present intuitive concepts of a primary mechanism of consciousness: The primary dynamic mechanism of attention is "soft focus - hard tokus" (tokus = buttocks). This concept has been subsequently reinforced for me daily, in the discipline of karate. It relates to the necessity during sparring of keeping an open global view of your interaction with your opponent, while aperiodically using your hips to focus precise defense-attack techniques. I then generalized this concept to describe the archetypal dynamics of perception (like "yin and yang") that gives feedback to partially control sensory processes, and that sculptures our cognitive and language structures. As such I believe these attention archetypes have molded our views of ourselves, of others, and of our biophysical universe. I have discussed these ideas in previous lectures to this seminar in past years.

As with any disciplined activity, most karate students and teachers, when doing their particular activity, are quite conservative, ruthless, and also quite emotional about any foreign intrusion into their physical or conceptual territory. Karate does offer a zen training in fundamentals of perceptual processes to those who seek it. I believe such metaphysical disciplines as zen are still superior to relatively underdeveloped academic attempts to understand and apply these processes to real life. Scientific systems do more clearly expose their true foundations, and therefore are easier to test, modify, or change. However, the price a heretic individual pays for attempting an actual change is the same in either system -- covert or overt excommunication. You must persist and presevere in your attempt to find a better belief system, or else readily accept theirs.

Objective Data

Without doubt, the most objective and testable findings about the empirical nature of brain functioning comes from the work done since the turn of this century by neuroscientists. It is consistent with my spiritual and intuitive framework to accept that most probably all of our concepts of mind are processed by our biophysical brains. Just how well we will do in developing a basic understanding of this functioning from basic physical principles may not be so easily resolved.

The personal aspects of science, i.e. the scientists, are pretty much the same as in other disciplines. They have their pet languages and mannerisms, but they function the same as all human beings, with the same low ratio of saints to sinners. However, the true strength of all science lies in its impersonal aspect. Knowledge, once properly formalized, is democratized and relatively free of dogmatic, esoteric, and petty gurus. In the neurosciences, the degree of conceptualization and formalism is relatively low, but the degree of accurate data collection is very high. So, after learning a fancy but precise language, a wealth of data becomes available, although it required a lot of difficult, clever, and sophisticated labor to obtain it. You can possess this data even if you don't agree with the politics of your nearest-neighbor neuroscientist, or even if he or she doesn't agree with you. You can read, go to seminars, even occasionally work with a neuroscientist, without penalty of pain. I've done this for over 10 years, and it's actually both fun and enlightening.

Some of the most important data collected which is relevant to the theory I'm developing, concerns the details of neuronal interactions in the human neocortex, the top of our brains. Tens of billions of neurons interact on time scales of milliseconds via tens of trillions of synaptic connections, like the crossings of many branches in a crowded forest. The quality of neuronal connections in the mammalian cortex is unique, with our most highly evolved human neocortex having the shortest ranged and most degenerate (duplicity) of interactions. Neurons interact by pulsing discharges of electrical energy transformed into chemical transmissions, initiated by accumulations of chemical transmissions from other neurons at their synaptic crossings. Initial conditions for cascades of these discharges may initiate from external sensory stimulation or from within the cerebral cortex itself. Perhaps even more remarkable is the rather uniform columnar units that spatially average the firing activities of their constituent neurons. In many of the hundred or so regions of cortex, these columns and their complexes have been identified as specific coordinators of sensory and motor activity. Entire regions that interact on time scales of hundreds of milliseconds have been mapped out as having specific sensory or motor functions. The two hemispheres have been strongly linked to information processing of simple stimuli akin to the concepts of yin-yang, of soft focus - hard tokus. Many statistical correlations have been made between behavioral activity and EEG recordings of electrical activity in the neocortex.

Analytic Paradigm

Anyone conversant with the language of a mathematical science such as physics, cannot help but respect such formalisms as invaluable tools to probe, reason, and to form viable, testable models of phenomena that otherwise would lie only as disjoint collectors' items of information. For over 20 years, our educational system has impressed upon me these ways of looking at nature. Concurrently, my professional activities have equally impressed upon me the metaphysical analogies of consciousness with the archetypal structures inherent in physics as developed by human physicists. For many years, I was fascinated to formulate these analogies along the same formal lines as modern physics, to somehow extract a model of consciousness that could go beyond vague description and equivocal innuendo, and be a testable precise model. In the past year, I have tried the opposite tack with more success, using the formal structures of physics to directly extract a reasonable model of brain activity that may explain some aspects of consciousness. I have drawn heavily on work done by other people, both inside and outside physics and the neurosciences.

First, the concept of neuronal interactions via synaptic transmissions was put into a mathematical analytic form that could foresee its input into more advanced formal structures. Then the concept of the column was similarly put into a mathematical form. Already some systematics of neuronal activity become clarified. Then the concept of a macroscopic region of millions of interacting columns was formulated by methods of modern statistical mechanics. In this form, a cortical region is described as the interplay between a driving electrical/chemical force and the inherently disordering fluctuations of columnar activity.

In its present form, this theory very much resembles other collective systems in physics, like magnetism and lasers. Some collective aspects may be solved directly by computers. Other fancy applications of recently advanced mathematical physics allows this theory to be put into an even more abstract, but simpler conceptual form better suited to study possible "phase transitions" in brain activity -- phase transitions from a relatively disordered state of functioning via local complex circuitry, to a relatively highly ordered cooperative state with new properties and structures. An exciting conjecture (intuited from other experiences mentioned above) is that focussed attention processes information via the local columnar circuitry, but that global attention and higher order patterns are processed via the global cooperative state. Furthermore, self-awareness may be describable as the interaction of the overall global pattern of "self" with the more local processing of detailed information.

More theory and calculations can and must be done, but even in its present form, experimental data can be described and predicted. This is what an analytic paradigm must do -- precisely describe the dynamics of a system from its most basic components and interactions, and predict and verify testable empirical consequences. It must do so in such a parsimonious way that the net result be aesthetically superior to the odd collection of facts it pulls together.

Personal/Societal Application

What should we expect from the correct blend of intuitive insight, objective data, and an analytic paradigm? Driven by spiritual and human purpose, some concrete applications should be realized. Yes, if this theory, or any other theory of brain function proven to be best, is correct, a better computer should be able to be designed and built.

However, full analysis is not always necessary to realize useful concrete applications. My own intuitions, probably many of which will be subsequently modified, were already being developed by applying ideas not yet fully analytically formulated. In 1970, after some success in developing academic teaching methods in physics, modelled after similar methods I developed for teaching dynamics of attention in karate, I started the Institute for the Study of Attention, now a subsidiary of Physical Studies Institute, to extend these ideas to other areas. Until 1978, I worked with other people to sponsor and teach in the ISA alternative junior and senior high school. The students and staff all greatly benefited from our 8 year project to help people develop attentional and learning skills in 30-odd academic, fine art, and physical disciplines.

This experience demonstrated to us the necessity of truly educating our young -- to educate them with the viable content of time tested disciplines with which they can intelligently venture forth with confidence to creatively explore new ideas. They must also be educated to become aware of the common mental and physical processes which they share with other humans. Such a common awareness not only can aid them to be more effective in learning and applying their knowledge, but it can also serve as a language with which they can better communicate and thereby appreciate their differences.

Conclusion

From the perceptions of one person and one pursuit, I have attempted to illustrate the importance of several disciplines and their attributes to investigate a phenomenon -- consciousness. Sometimes the processes of investigation of one person can encompass most of these attributes; sometimes specific tasks or attitudes permit only a group, or only many groups of people to so encompass them. Obviously the person is richer for exploring as many as possible, and society requires exploration of all to approach an understanding of nature.

IIIC. Other Publications

If you are interested in following up some of these ideas, I have published some of relatively non-technical papers. Two recent papers are published in the *Journal for Social and Biological Studies,* Volume 4 (1981), a publication of Academic Press Inc. (London) Limited, devoted to such interdisciplinary research. After looking at these papers in your local college library and if you cannot get copies made there, or if you cannot find these papers, you can obtain copies from Physical Studies Institute by writing to us and including $2.50 each to cover costs incurred for copying, postage, and handling:

PSI
Drawer W
Solana Beach, CA 92075

The titles and abstracts of these papers are:

IIIC-1. "Attention, physics and teaching"

A specific physics problem format has been successful in helping students to develop strategies in solving standard physics problems. The basic structure of this format simultaneously presents alternative patterns of possible solutions/approaches with a correlated package of several related facts/criteria that can be utilized as a foundation to construct a formal analysis of the problem.

p. 225-235

IIIC-2. "Towards a unified brain theory"

An approach to collective aspects of the neocortical system is formulated by methods of modern non-equilibrium statistical mechanics. Microscopic neuronal synaptic interactions are first spatially averaged over columnar domains. These spatially ordered domains include well formulated fluctuations that retain contact with the original synaptic parameters. They are also a suitable substrate for macroscopic spatial-temporal regions described by Fokker-Planck and Lagrangian formalisms. This development clarifies similarities and differences among previous studies, suggests new analytically supported insights into neocritical function and permits future approximation or elaboration within current paradigms of collective systems.

p. 211-224